Dialogue in the Philosophy of Education

The Coordinated Teacher Preparation Series
Under the Editorship of
Donald E. Orlosky
University of South Florida

Dialogue in the Philosophy of Education

Howard Ozmon
Virginia Commonwealth University

Charles E. Merrill Publishing Company
A Bell & Howell Company
Columbus, Ohio

Acknowledgments

I would like to thank the following for their help in commenting upon this book during various stages of its development: Davele Bursor, Tom Huber, S. H. Hardy, Frances Briggs, Walter Coppedge, and Bertram Bandman. I would also like to thank Jim Bailey for his assistance in editing and typing the manuscript in its final form.

International Standard Book Number: 0-675-09155-1
Library of Congress Catalog Card Number: 74-181354
1 2 3 4 5 6 7 8 9 10 – 75 74 73 72

Printed in the United States of America

Preface

This book was written for the purpose of acquainting students with educational philosophy. Unlike long treatises on the subject, however, which often necessitate the student's keeping a finger on one philosophy while trying to compare it with the next, the philosophies in this book are presented in dialogue form. There are many advantages to this kind of approach. To begin with, it is the kind of real discussion that might take place between educational philosophers, and it enables the student to encounter rebuttals made by philosophers of different persuasions during each step of the discussion. Basically, I have endeavored to present the major beliefs of six different educational philosophies: perennialism, essentialism, progressivism, reconstructionism, behavioral engineering, and existentialism. There are some similarities among these philosophies, but there are also many differences, and I have attempted to make these differences clear through a constant on-going challenge of varying viewpoints.

I feel that the use of the dialogue as a method in education has been sadly neglected even though the most brilliant educational treatise ever written, Plato's *Republic,* was done in this fashion. I think that the dialogue serves not only to present ideas, but also action. One tends to be drawn in more as a participant than in any other style of writing.

I realized from the outset that although I might try to present each philosophy fairly, it would be impossible for me to present a view that would satisfy all educational philosophers, and I accepted that fate at the start of writing this book. Should the student be tempted to cry out that the perennialist should not have said this or that, or that the existentialist gave a stupid reply, I will not be too chagrined, for the purpose of this book, after all, is to encourage people to think and not to accept points of view from whatever source blindly.

I have never believed that a study of educational philosophy was a dull affair, but I must say that this view was obtained only with some effort, after being exposed to some very dull books and some very dull professors on the subject. I have tried here to show the passion it can generate among those who have devoted their lives to arguing philosophical positions, and to show also the importance of considering philosophical perspectives with regard to the problems of education and society.

Contents

Introduction

Someone once said that the only unique contributions that the United States has made to the world are jazz and plumbing. We are certainly not in the forefront of world civilizations when it comes to great music, unforgettable literature, and undying art. Yet, we are a young nation only a few centuries old, whereas the European nations have been cultivating such arts for a long time. Most of what we have in the way of great art in America is an import. We have museums and art galleries filled with the discoveries of English and Spanish explorers, music that was written in Austria, literature from Russia, and art from Italy. The case is no different with philosophy. Most of our philosophies are imports, too, which come to us from Greece, France, Germany, England, China, and other places. They have names, at least in Western philosophy, like Idealism and Realism (which may be traced back to ancient Greece) and Existentialism (which received its major thrust in France and Germany). Even Pragmatism and Behaviorism,* which are thought of as American philosophies, have their roots in such diverse places, respectively, as England (with the empirical movement) and Russia (with the work of Pavlov).

It is interesting to note that almost every major philosopher wrote about education in one way or another, and one finds it extensively treated by Plato and Aristotle, St. Thomas Aquinas, Bacon, Locke, Rousseau, Kant, Marx, Dewey, and Buber. Plato, for example, makes education the foundation of the *Republic,* and it would be impossible to separate Plato's ideas about education from his ideas on economics, politics, and religion. With most philosophers, their ideas on education are intrinsically and integrally related to their basic philosophies, and are either an essential part of its development or an outgrowth of it.

---

*Behaviorism is generally looked upon more as a psychological position than as a philosophical one. It is a position, however, that has great philosophical implications for education, particularly through the work of J. B. Watson and B. F. Skinner.

When one begins to philosophize, he may do so for a variety of reasons: to design ideal states as Plato did; to give advice as in Machiavelli's *The Prince;* to attempt an understanding and interpretation of the world we live in, as suggested by St. Thomas, Hegel, and Marx; to synthesize knowledge such as we find in Kant; to criticize existing institutions as Voltaire did; or to provide some impetus to action as in the philosophies of Sartre and Dewey. There are many reasons for philosophizing just as there are many philosophies, and philosophies have been seen from many different vantage points. Educational ideas, too, can be seen in terms of particular purposes: For Plato, education is to lead man to the World of Ideas; for St. Augustine and St. Thomas, philosophy assists man on his road to heaven and salvation; for Marx, it leads to the development of "social consciousness"; and for many modern philosophers, philosophy is utilized as a way of obtaining technical skill, developing a critical attitude, or an awareness of oneself and others.

Although we are not a "philosophic" nation, we do have many accomplishments in scientific and technical fields which need to be looked at philosophically and which have philosophical meaning not only for ourselves but for the rest of the world as well. Perhaps this is because, traditionally, we have held the man of action in higher esteem than the thinking man. We are an action-oriented nation but have failed to see that this too represents a certain philosophical attitude, and one that necessitates a great deal of self-analysis. In education we have accomplished many remarkable things. We have, for the first time in history, attempted a massive program of trying to educate everyone to the limits of his potential. We have an extensive system of higher education, and education has been utilized as a means of obliterating class and racial differences, a process still unheard of in many nations that consider themselves advanced and progressive. Yet, we do have a sense of uneasiness about what we have so far accomplished as well as what we should aim toward in the future. We have failed—and it has been the mark of our age—to keep wisdom at pace with our technical advancements. We need to reexamine just what our purposes and goals should be in this country, and this necessitates a rethinking of methods and purposes in education as well.

It has been said that everything reflects a philosophy of some sort, but I believe this is a gross overgeneralization. Attitudes and ideas may reflect many different philosophies at once, or what we mean by philosophy may even be, and often is, disjointed and even contradictory thinking, which certainly is not philosophy in terms of logical coherent thought. It is true that people can tend to their everyday functions in business, education, or social affairs, with little or no understanding of philosophy or philosophical thinking, but it seems to me that some knowledge of philosophy can be of inestimable value in refining and enlarging what we do. I know many educators, for example, who arrived late in life at some knowledge of philosophy that was of great value to them in developing a new perspective toward their day-to-day activities in education. Yet, even now, we continue to emphasize method and action in education rather than thought and direction. I am not opposed to either of these, but I do think we need to see a complementarity between thought and action that is sadly neglected in present-day life. In education today, I think we are in serious danger of turning out educational plumbers, i.e., people who have acquired a certain expertise and know-how in doing things, but do not know why they are doing them or even if they should be done. In some schools of education, courses in the philosophy of education are not taught because of a feeling that they either tend to slow down the process or because they confuse the student by raising questions rather than getting him to accept ready-made answers. I do not think that either of these charges is necessarily true, but regardless of whether they are or not, I think we desperately need to know what we are doing and why we are doing it, and a study of philosophical thinking can assist us in this process better than anything else.

Another argument often advanced against studies in philosophy is: Why should one study philosophy when philosophers themselves do not agree with each other? But this argument overlooks two valuable points: First of all, many philosophers have agreed with each other, and out of such agreement rose great philosophical systems such as Stoicism, Epicureanism, Christianity, and Communism. Philosophers, like anyone else should, however, try to improve their thinking, and this can only be done by posing new questions, and hopefully, arriving at new answers. In this book, for example, the emphasis seems to be on disagreement, but I think the perceptive reader will see that there are many areas of agreement as well, and the debate between philosophers is not one intended for the purpose of winning an argument as much as it is a way of improving how one thinks.

Critique

I should like to present five major philosophical positions that have significant ramifications for educational philosophy. They are: Idealism, Realism, Pragmatism, Existentialism, and Behaviorism.

Idealism. This is a philosophical system which maintains that reality is composed of ideas. Idealism emphasizes mind, soul, and spirit, rather than a material world. Some important Idealists were Plato, Berkeley, and Hegel.

Realism. As a philosophy Realism is the belief that there is a reality independent of men's minds, and that ideas and things do not necessarily depend on man's thinking for objectivity. Some important Realists were Aristotle, St. Thomas, and Spinoza.

Pragmatism. This philosophy maintains that minds are to be used for solving problems and that the practical consequences of ideas can determine their value and meaning. Pragmatists attempt to apply the scientific method humanistically to philosophical thinking. Some important Pragmatists were William James and John Dewey.

Existentialism. This is a philosophy devoted to describing and evaluating "the human condition." Existential philosophy is primarily concerned with man's existence. The two major kinds of existentialism are: Christian existentialism as represented by Kierkegaard, Jaspers, and Marcel; and atheistic existentialism as represented by Sartre, Camus, Nietzsche, and Heidegger.

Behaviorism. Behaviorism represents an attempt to control human behavior through a system of rewards and punishments referred to, respectively, as positive and aversive reinforcement. Although some behaviorists do not utilize punishment, this is by no means universal among all behaviorists. Some important behaviorists are Pavlov, Watson, and Skinner.

These five philosophical positions, some of which have developed over a long span of time, have resulted in specific educational philosophies as follow:

Philosophy	*Educational Philosophy*
Idealism	⟵⟶ Perennialism
Realism	⟵⟶ Essentialism
Pragmatism	⟵⟶ Progressivism
	Reconstructionism
Existentialism	⟵⟶ Existentialism
Behaviorism	⟵⟶ Behavioral Engineering

Something may now be said about each of these educational philosophies in turn:

Perennialism.   Perennialism as an educational philosophy deals with that which is lasting. It tends, therefore, to emphasize art and science that has weathered the test of time and which has become an integral part of human history. It promotes a literary or "Great Books" approach to human learning, and utilizes seminars and discussions as appropriate ways to deal with the best that has been thought in the world. Underlying this philosophy is the notion that we should seek to discover those laws and ideas that have proven value to the world in which we live. The function of education, therefore, is to learn those things that have already been discovered about the world and to search for new truths whenever possible. Primarily, Perennialists see their task as one of encouraging people to become "philosophically-minded." Some major Perennialists in education are Adler, Hutchins, and Maritain.

Essentialism.   Essentialism deals with essentials or basic things that people should know not only to be fully aware of the world in which they live, but that are also necessary for human survival. Primarily, this educational philosophy emphasizes fact-data such as the three "R's" in one's early learning experiences, followed by concentrated studies in mathematics, history, and science. Essentialists are greatly concerned that education be rigorous and efficient, and they are greatly disturbed by fads and frills that they feel pervade much of what passes for education. Essentialists feel that mental discipline should be utilized to learn basic information about the world in which we live, and, primarily, they are interested in turning out specialists who can deal with and advance the kind of technical society in which we live. Some important essentialists in education are Koerner, Rafferty, and Rickover.

Progressivism. Progressivists would like to see people become good problem-solvers. The Progressivist is opposed to any search for absolute truth whether it be in philosophy or science, and is more interested that people take a pragmatic attitude toward life by discovering things that work and are useful. Education for the Progressivist is not product but process. He is trying to turn out people who can face current or future problems and solve them with a great deal of skill. Progressivists promote a synoptic approach toward education with a corresponding effort to unite school and society in ways to better educate and humanize people. Progressivism is student-centered in that it encourages educators to motivate students toward learning by providing meaningful tasks that they can solve in an atmosphere that is both pleasurable and democratic. Progressivism is experimental by nature and seeks to promote useful changes in man and society. Some important Progressivists in education include Dewey, Kilpatrick, Bode, and Childs.

Reconstructionism. Reconstructionists promote the use of problem-solving, but feel that any problem-solving ability that is developed should be geared toward solving significant social problems. They are critical of what they consider too much "life adjustment" in the approach of many Progressivists, and feel that we need to think of education in terms of both short- and long-range goals. Reconstructionists feel that a utopian approach toward education is useful as a way of stimulating people to think about a better world that they can help to create. Reconstructionists deemphasize an academic approach to education in favor of getting people to become change-agents by participating directly in the affairs of life. Important Reconstructionists in education include Counts and Brameld.

Existentialism. Existentialism, as an educational philosophy, places its emphasis upon the individual. Existentialists are primarily concerned with life as it is and not with its abstract qualities. They feel that we should use education as a way of encouraging people to become more involved in life as well as committed to action. They feel that the individual should seek for self-improvement in an ever-changing world. Existentialists emphasize an "I-Thou"* approach to education in which everyone is involved in the educational process as both teacher and learner. They promote a humanistic "inner-directed" approach to education such as that suggested by Carl Rog-

---

*For a fuller discussion of the "I-Thou" concept the student is referred to *I and Thou* by Martin Buber (New York: Charles Scribner's Sons, 1958). Basically, Buber feels that people should experience "I-Thou" relationships where they treat each other as persons, rather than "I-It" relationships in which people are treated as objects.

ers that allows students freedom of choice in terms of curriculum and educational outcome. Some modern educational existentialists are Buber, Neill, Kneller, and Morris.

Behavioral Engineering.   Behavioral engineering is an educational philosophy that utilizes the methods of conditioning as a way of directing human behavior. Behavioral engineers feel that much of human behavior reflects attitudes and actions already conditioned by the environment, and that these attitudes and actions should be engineered along paths that are more useful and productive. They would like to see educators develop the kind of environment in schools whereby individuals are encouraged through rewards and punishments toward those things that will help best to benefit themselves and others. Promoters of the use of behavioral engineering in education include Skinner, Watson, Bereiter, and Engleman.

* * * *

This introduction was provided to give the reader some kind of basic orientation toward the six philosophies he will encounter in the following pages. Although the dialogue is presented in a way which does not necessitate any prior knowledge of philosophy or philosophy of education, it is hoped that the additional information here will make the ideas you encounter that much more meaningful and significant.

Dramatis Personae *

The perennialist – – – – – – – Pennington
The essentialist – – – – – – – – Estabrook
The progressivist – – – – – – – Price
The reconstructionist – – – – Reed
The existentialist – – – – – – – Extan
The behavioral engineer – – Beattie
The man from EDCO – – – Edwards

---

*To help simplify identification, the reader will note that each character's name contains the first two letters of the educational philosophy he represents.

1

The First Day

Onc by one, six men filed into the conference room. They waited nervously, unknown to each other, not even knowing why they had been called together. Suddenly, a small, well-dressed man carrying an attaché case entered and went to the head of the table. He did not look up until he had opened the attaché case and laid several pieces of paper on the table in front of him. Then his eyes surveyed the group as he spoke.

"Gentlemen, my name is Edwards. I know you are wondering why you are here. As you know, EDCO Corporation is one of the leading systems analysts in the field of education. Accordingly, we feel the need for a constant on-going analysis of our own programs, and we have brought you together as the foremost authorities on educational philosophy in America." He looked at each man in turn as he identified them by name and position: perennialist (Pennington), essentialist (Estabrook), progressivist (Price), reconstructionist (Reed), existentialist (Extan), and behavioral engineer (Beattie).

Edwards continued: "We have gotten you together to analyze and compare your philosophics of education so that we can reassess the policies and programs of our company in the light of your thinking. We do not necessarily desire that you reach agreement, but we would like to know where you do agree and where you do not. In short, gentlemen, we feel that educational philosophy is important and that it should be the first step in formulating better aims and methods for education. Since I feel that my presence here might be an inhibiting factor, I shall leave you free to approach this matter in any way you deem fit. We do have a continuous tape running, however, which will record your conversation for future study. Are there any questions?"

Pennington looked up and coughed slightly, his aquiline features glinting from the morning light. "We are to propose a philosophy for American education?"

"Not necessarily," said the EDCO representative. "We realize that there probably can not be any one educational philosophy, that everything is probably eclectic in some way. What we want is some critical and intensive thinking about the process of American education. We'll draw our own conclusions as to what we will or will not accept, after you complete your deliberations."

Estabrook leveled his steel blue eyes at Edwards and said: "You don't want clear-cut answers?"

"We want hard thinking. And we think you are the men to do it."

Professor Beattie, the behavioral engineer, doodled with his pencil a bit longer before he spoke. "How long have we . . . to do this?"

"As long as you want," replied Edwards. "We have arranged with your various institutions for an indefinite stay. Take as long as you want."

"Are we to stay here?" asked Extan, who had already taken his tie off.

"No, go wherever you want," replied Edwards. "We just want some good, hard thinking."

"I don't know how much we can do in a short time," said Reed.

"Do what you can," he answered. "We'll try to be patient." Concluding this statement, Edwards closed his attaché case and hurried briskly out of the room, leaving it quietly hushed.

"The issue seems clear," said Estabrook. "Let's try to come up with something."

"Where shall we begin?" asked Beattie.

"I propose we agree on a set of values to guide the discussion," said Pennington.

"Opposed," replied Reed, tapping his finger quietly on the desk. "Let's try to be open-ended."

"I agree," said Price. "Let's don't pin ourselves down to a pat way of thinking."

"I agree with Pennington," said Estabrook. "We must decide upon basic things first."

There was a moment of silence and they all looked at Extan to break the deadlock.

Finally Extan spoke, "I propose we begin and then examine that issue later."

"Well, where shall we start, then?" asked Estabrook.

"Let's discuss a concrete issue like federal aid to education," said Price, "and see if we can come up with any answers."

"Let's not get bogged down in side issues," said Pennington. "What we need to do is to develop a set of guidelines, and then we can apply these guidelines to any issue."

"But all instances are different," stated Extan with some feeling.

"Yes, but not that different," said Estabrook. "We can at least discuss basic ideas."

"I think the broader issues should come first," said Reed. "Then we can get down to the minor ones."

"Well, then," questioned Pennington, "what is philosophy of education?"

"Something to teach people how to problem-solve," replied Price.

"Yes, but toward what end?" asked the reconstructionist. "I mean we have a lot of problem-solvers around today, yet the world is in quite a mess. Maybe we need to think about what kind of world we want first."

"You can have any kind of world you want," countered Beattie. "We have techniques at our disposal to shape both the world and the people. All we need is some sort of go-ahead."

"I think there has been too much shaping already," said Extan.

"Perhaps," replied Beattie, "but people are going to be shaped anyway. It's just a matter of deciding who is going to shape them."

"People should shape themselves," offered the existentialist.

"But they will," replied Beattie. "We'll condition them to do just that."

"I am not opposed to conditioning," Reed stated firmly, "but I do think we should explore what kind of world we want to condition them toward."

"Man is not a machine," said Pennington. "Yet you want to treat him as one. What we really need to do is to deal with those aspects of man that are truly human, such as his ability to think, to reason. Why do you want to take away man's ability to reason?"

"Why do you think machines are so detrimental?" asked Beattie. "Machines are there to help man, not to hurt him."

"Though they sometimes do," replied Extan, "I'm afraid that technology often tends to obscure basic human qualities, and tends to make people act like machines."

"We've been sitting here for twenty minutes and haven't gotten anything done yet," said Estabrook. "If we really hope to accomplish something we've got to structure this whole discussion in a way to generate some concrete results."

"But we've already agreed to be open-ended," Pennington answered. "You can't put philosophical concepts in any kind of neat little package. They're too broad for that."

"The real trouble with education," said Estabrook, "is that we've strayed away from teaching the things that are really important: the three 'R's,' basic facts, and all that."

"But what are facts?" asked Price. "Facts change. The facts our parents learned are not the same facts we teach today. Yet, we still have problems. We need to teach people how to solve problems, not learn facts."

"I don't like the word 'fact' either," said Pennington sternly. "I know some of you will think this old-fashioned, but I think we need to gear our educational programs toward seeking Truth, or at least those things that are more lasting."

"That's what's causing all the problems now," stated Price. "It's all this truth seeking. Let's forget about truth and talk more about probability and likelihood!"

"All this talk about facts, truth, and problem-solving leaves me cold," said Extan. "Whatever happened to man? Somehow he gets submerged in all your methods, categories, and theories."

"Man is only what we make him," replied Beattie. "He doesn't really have any identity except what we give him. By controlling his experiences we control what he is."

"Although I detect some bit of humanism in what the perennialist says, I must say that I don't see too much of it in the rest of you," replied Extan. "Man is no puppet to be manipulated by your educational theories. Why, you make education out to be something that gobbles up man!"

"I wish that were true," said Estabrook. "But actually I think most of the time we don't have too much effect one way or the other. I wouldn't object to all this conditioning and problem-solving if it were getting us somewhere, but right now we're just kind of floundering."

"I think that the world to come needs some humanistic values built into it," said Reed. "We need some kind of direction. We can't just let man go his own anarchic way as the existentialist seems to suggest."

"There is order in everything," said Pennington. He looked around the room and then he continued: "We perennialists are much older than any of you in the business of educational philosophy. We go back to Plato, to Aristotle, St. Augustine, and St. Thomas, not to mention a whole list of modern thinkers like Robert Hutchins and Mortimer Adler. We think that man should concentrate on those ideas that are more or less permanent—those that have weathered the test of time. We strongly promote the great books, the classics in general, and we feel that American education should structure itself around those ideas that have been found to be the most important ones for mankind. I guess that gives a capsule summary of what we believe."

"We essentialists also feel that some ideas are more important than others," said Estabrook, "but primarily we feel that we need scientific answers rather than philosophical ones. We live in a world where our very survival may be at stake, and where we need answers to solve our growing technological problems. We feel that if people are equipped with the basic facts we know about our universe, then they will be able to meet any of the challenges that face them."

"I think facts have their place," said Price, "but situations are never the same and the same facts don't always apply. There is, for example, little advantage in knowing the facts of history as a way of helping us to solve our current difficulties. Progressivists think, however, that if people are encouraged to be good problem-solvers, then they will be able to meet whatever challenges there are and overcome them."

"As I have stated before, I am all in favor of problem-solving," said Reed. "But I also feel that we need to have some kind of utopian vision of what we're problem-solving toward. One might say, for example, that the Nazis were good problem-solvers, but they led the world in a direction that not many of us would care to go. We need to think about change in some directional sense that I do not find clarified in the progressive approach, but is developed in reconstructionism."

"Basically," said Extan, "we existentialists believe in the authentic man; a man who becomes an individual through his own free commitment to action. We are alarmed by institutions and systems that delimit the power of man to control his own destiny, and we feel that man needs to assert his right to control his own life. This is not without some pain and difficulty, but we feel that it is a necessary part of being a true individual. We are opposed to educational programs that stuff either facts, truth, or problem-solving down a student's throat. We feel that the individual himself should decide what he wants to obtain out of his education or even if he is to be educated."

"I must take serious issue with such a view of man," replied Beattie. "Studies with pigeons, as well as man have shown that animals behave as they are reinforced to behave. By controlling the reward mechanisms that guide human behavior we in turn guide man. This view may not make one happy, but it is based on a great deal of investigation. Since man is not free but controlled by a vast array of forces which he may not know, we feel that it is quite appropriate to utilize these controlling mechanisms in ways that make man better. For many years we have talked of making man more loving and humane. Yet every method to do this has failed. Now, through engineering his behavior and rewarding him for peace-like activities we can actually make him become a peaceful individual."

"Now that we've heard the gist of our philosophies," said Price, glancing at each man in turn, "I think it would be most fruitful if we would now delineate how we would deal with specific educational problems or issues. What shall we take?"

"The role of the teacher," Pennington answered quickly.

"The individual," added Extan.

"Society," replied Reed.

Estabrook said in a thoughtful tone, "I think these are all too vague. Let's deal with an issue such as strengthening American education."

"How about," said Beattie, "the kind of person we want to turn out? I think that all of us have an interest in this and that it would in turn deal with the other issues that have been mentioned."

There was general agreement on this point, and Pennington called again to be heard.

"The kind of person that we want to see turned out is the philosophically-oriented person," he said. "We want someone who has wisdom; who can see the broader issues of humanity and deal with them."

"Sometimes the broader issues obscure the more immediate issues," Price stated.

"Or shed light upon them," added Reed. "I agree that we should consider the broader issues and I do feel that we have to think about turning out people who are philosophically-oriented, but I think that they should be motivated toward change rather than toward the kind of staticism the perennialist promotes."

"We would like to develop a scientifically-oriented person," said Estabrook. "We think that technological expertise is important and essential. Philosophy bakes no bread, but technological expertise does."

"I don't like either your philosophical person or your scientific one," replied Extan. "I think you would do better to think of a person without any label. Let people become themselves, individuals, rather than pushing them toward some predetermined goal."

"But what is a person?" asked Beattie. "He's a kind of superma-chine with things that can be programmed. When you leave him alone he's nothing. You have to direct him for his own good. Even your 'individual' is one who has been conditioned to be one."

"You know," said Price, "this is all interesting, but I doubt if we are really fulfilling the assignment. We know that we have a lot of differ-ences, but how about our similarities? There must be some things we agree on, or some of us anyway."

"I think so," said Extan. "At least I agree with you that we need to concern ourselves with present problems and do something about them, though I do think you are a little more optimistic about results than I am."

"Of course I'm all for solving contemporary problems too," replied Reed, "but I think you need to have some sort of goals ahead of you."

"We're all concerned with contemporary problems to some ex-tent," said the essentialist. "That's not the point. The thing is, how do you solve them? We feel that one needs to know things like science, history, and the like, in order to solve them."

"Yes, but you only solve them in a very limited way," offered Pennington. "Too often both you and Price suggest things that only lead to further problems. I agree with the reconstructionist that you need a vision, but I also feel that vision often exists more in light of the wisdom of the past than that which is with us or before us. We don't know what the future will bring, but we do know what the past has been."

"In a way then," said Beattie, "I suppose you could say that the progressivist, the essentialist, the existentialist, and myself are all very much concerned with the now, while the reconstructionist is concerned more with the future, and the perennialist with the past."

"That's a very general statement," replied Reed with a shake of his head. "I already said I was concerned with present problems. If you mean more exclusively concerned, I suppose I would have to go along with that."

"We perennialists are also concerned with the present problems," countered Pennington. "But generally we find that present problems are really old problems in new guises. That's why it's important to know how they were dealt with before."

"I should like to ask Reed what he as a reconstructionist sees in the future," said Estabrook.

Reed replied, "I have certain ideas about what the future may be or can be like, and that helps me to think more constructively in the present. For example, we reconstructionists would like to see a world without war, hunger or poverty. We think that education could assist man in reaching such a world."

"I think all of us would like to have those things," answered Beattie, "but how will you get them? Not by extending any of the previous methods you've used. Besides we've always had education, and we could make a good point that it is education that has been used to make men warlike, to enable them to cheat others, and to keep people in slavery. We feel that not only education, but man must be changed, and we are now embarking on methods which enable us to do just that."

"Conditioning does not frighten me," said Reed. "Indeed, I see a great place for it in the world of the future. But we are concerned that it be utilized humanistically, and that is one of the problems that must be worked out."

"I believe," said Estabrook, "that it was mentioned before that one could be conditioned to be free, creative, loving, and so on. I do not deny that conditioning is an effective method for doing this, but I do wonder about the fact that the individual is not doing it himself, but rather that it is being done to him by others."

"One cannot be conditioned to reach truth," stated Pennington emphatically, "or to arrive at wisdom. If we have wisdom, why isn't it in your conditioning mechanisms?"

"I will admit that there is and has been a great scarcity of wisdom in the world," replied Beattie, "but part of the reason is because man has not been conditioned to seek wisdom, but to buy products, to spend his time foolishly, or in some sensuous pursuit. We can even condition people to become philosophers, or to seek for truth, whatever that means."

"Like the progressivist," said Estabrook, "all this truth business leaves me cold. We're not looking for truth. We're looking for things that are practical, things that you can use."

"I am certainly not against things that are useful," said Pennington, "but I do think we should keep in mind that there are higher things than immediate problems. I think we should ask ourselves why we are here, and what we should be doing."

"A perfect example of a pseudo-problem," stated Price. "You know that we can never come to any definitive answers regarding such questions."

"Yes, I realize that," answered Pennington. "It is not the answers we are so much concerned with, as with the value of seeking such answers. We think that man should stretch himself, and even if the answers are not immediately forthcoming, he should try to reach them. This is the very definition of philosophy—the love of truth and the search for wisdom."

"I agree with Price," responded Estabrook. "Such metaphysical questions are time-consuming and end in nothing. If anything they tend to confuse students so that they don't get their proper work done."

"We believe in the value of such confusion," said Pennington. "The problem today is that everyone is so cocksure of what he knows and what he is doing. Everyone is so self-satisfied with his little piece of specialized knowledge. No one wants to put it all together, to try to see the whole rather than some tiny part. I agree it's a lot more difficult but so much more important."

"Although no one has ever referred to me as a metaphysician," said Reed, "I do believe that there is great value in looking at the whole. We need to try to see all of our knowledge as one unified whole and then to direct it toward certain desired ends. This demands some amount of speculation, which is what Pennington is talking about."

"All this talk about arriving at knowledge, building up knowledge, and the orderly process of knowledge is a most ridiculous thing," exploded Extan. "I hear you, but no one really talks about man, man not only as a thinker, or philosopher, but man as he is, man in all of his nakedness, as well as his glory."

"Yes," said Pennington, "but you sometimes dwell on the nakedness. We know it's there, but we feel that we need to inspire man, to make him go beyond the purely human."

"That's a contradiction in terms," said Extan. "Besides, many times in the past we neglected what is truly human and natural, and look at the result. You can't cover man up with a veneer of civilization and say that that's it. Man will prevail."

"It is good that the existentialist is here," said Beattie. "It is true that we do sometimes tend to forget the human side of man, and human needs, but I will go one step further and say that we need to consider the animal side of man, and the animal side is one which reacts in very predictable ways. We can utilize man's animal side to take him beyond the purely animal."

"And in so doing destroy what is truly man," replied Extan. "Probably, from my point of view, you have the most dangerous philosophy of all. We already know how technology has dehumanized man, and you are talking about going further. You won't be satisfied until you take what is human or animal about man and turn it into some kind of superelectronic machine that you can just plug in and it begins to behave."

"I must say that I am equally disturbed about this," responded Price. "We have not been opposed to technological advances in education. Far from it. But on the other hand we have always championed a democratic attitude toward education, an attitude which insists that individuals be treated as individuals so that they determine their own goals and interests. The existentialist is worried over a loss of identity and humanness. We are too, in light of the democratic attitude we hold about man."

"If I may add a word to that," said Extan. "We are not so concerned because it may be democratic, but because we are interested in developing the human side of man. We hold no allegiance to any particular kind of social or political philosophy."

"We are equally concerned," said Pennington. "Most of the works that we are interested in seeing students use fall into that category known as the humanities. In effect, they deal with the human side of man."

"Yes, that sounds very nice," said Price. "Only it does seem to me that the books you use tend to get more important than the person. Many of the people I know who are specialists in the humanities are very inhumane in their personal lives."

"Yes, I'm afraid the great ideas tend to overshadow the person," replied the reconstructionist. "And it also tends to lead to an elitist program of education, i.e., the person who knows the most great ideas is the best."

"But aren't we all elitists to some extent?" queried Estabrook. "I mean we favor the one who knows the most facts, the problem-solver rates high the good problem-solver, the existentialist prefers the one who introspects best, the reconstructionist values the best builder."

"That may be true for the rest of you," said Extan. "But it is certainly not true for me. We do not put a value on human beings because of their special knowledge or degrees, but because of their humanness. This is to say that we would rate a truck driver equal to a professor if both had chosen and committed themselves to their occupation."

"What we behavioral engineers would like to think," offered Beattie, "is that there are various jobs to do, and that we can prepare individuals for each particular kind of work. If the work is important then there is an equalizing factor there, though we do know that different kinds of work require differing degrees of intelligence and skill."

"I'm afraid that existentialists do not put such an emphasis on work, or on building the new society, as you do," said Extan. "We feel that man is of ultimate value in and of himself. It is what he chooses to do that is the most important thing—that it is his own free choice."

"The only thing that bothers me," said Reed, "and here I think I am speaking for some of the others as well, is that your views lead to a kind of anarchy in society—in people doing their own thing. Though I feel that I have outgrown my Puritan attitude toward work as a necessary moral thing, I do wonder at the results of your philosophy, and whether or not you foresee them yourself."

"Yes," replied Pennington, "not only is your philosophy anarchic but perhaps even distressingly human. I'm afraid that if we followed your philosophy to its lengths we would only be concerned with eating, sleeping, sex, and other animal things. Where is there room for the spiritual side of man?"

"Could I suggest," said Price, "that you rephrase your question to say the religious side of man? 'Spiritual' implies a certain occult influence."

"I don't care whether you call it spiritual or religious," said the perennialist. "I just want to know where one finds it in existential philosophy?"

"I find the question completely irrelevant," replied Extan. "There is nothing 'religious' or 'spiritual' in the world, though certainly man can create something which he calls religious or spiritual."

"I do not see where we have to posit any such qualities," said Beattie. "They are completely unnecessary, though as Extan points out, we can create so-called spiritual or religious attitudes."

"Gentlemen," said Reed, "I think we are going somewhat astray. Just how is all of this related to our educational philosophies?"

"Since I brought it up," said Pennington, "I think that it is quite relevant, for some of you seem to forget that being human means more than being just an animal or a machine. It means being somewhat of an angelic creature, and we believe there should be education for the angel side of man as well as for his other parts."

"Just what is this 'angel side'?" asked Beattie.

"It is man's reasoning ability," replied Pennington. "Something that transcends all of your ideas on gadgetry, and is probably something you can't understand."

"I would not be opposed," said Extan, "to admitting certain so-called religious values like courage, steadfastness, nobility, and the like, but I think it is true that when you deify anything, even reason, you begin to blind yourself to human possibilities. We feel that reason is quite suspect, and that most of the reasoning that man does is really what you might call rationalization, i.e., after the fact. We feel that much of what man does is based on emotion or instinct, and that man only uses reason to justify why he does it."

"While admitting that reason may err," said Price, "the probability of our answers being sound is much more likely when we use reason than when we don't."

"Yes, you often use reason to justify reason, which is rather circular," mused Extan. "For example, you believe in problem-solving. But what does it mean to solve a problem? I mean, how do you know it's solved? Suppose I have financial problems and I rob a bank; that solves my problem doesn't it?"

"Yes, temporarily," admitted the progressivist, "but you may incur more difficult problems through such a method."

"That's exactly my point," said Extan. "How can you be sure at any point that the problem is solved, completely solved?"

"I think we have to admit that we can't in any absolute way," responded Price. "But we never claimed to have any kind of infallible method. We simply try to make people aware of the consequences of their actions."

"Yes, I know that," said the existentialist, "but you do talk about problems being solved and all that. Really, I think we must say that all problem-solving is merely a holding operation."

"That is exactly the point I have been trying to make," exclaimed Reed. "In any kind of problem-solving there must be an awareness of ends to make problem-solving really meaningful and purposive."

"Yes, but I find your proposal equally distressing," replied Extan, "because there are no certain goals or purposes inherent in the nature of man. Man can create and go in any direction he chooses."

"That's true," said Reed. "We don't feel that goals are any more infallible than problem-solving. Goals may be changed at any time. We feel that anything that man does can only be meaningful in terms of some larger design."

"While the perennialist looks to the past, you look to the future," said Extan. "Although the differences are in many ways very great, we side much more with the essentialist and the progressivist in looking at things as they are at the present time."

"If you mean that we wish to apply some of the ideas of the past to the present you are quite correct," said Pennington, "but I really doubt that any of us fit in the tight little compartments you've made for us."

"On the contrary, I think you are all quite complex," replied Extan. "It is only that we younger philosophers feel a great need to put our feelings in rather strong terms."

"A while back Price tried to pull us to order in discussing our philosophies," said Reed, "but I'm afraid we've gone astray again."

"Perhaps we might try a new tack," said Estabrook. "Why don't we each try to establish what kinds of schools we would like to see and maybe that will shed more light on our philosophies."

"Yes," said Extan, "I think that would be much more beneficial than the kind of web spinning we've been doing."

"Let Pennington go first as before," said Beattie, "and we'll follow in the same order."

"Very well," said Pennington. "To begin with, the kind of school that I envision will be in an aesthetically designed environment, perhaps even with fountains and places for contemplation. The whole atmosphere will be one pervaded with learning and the love of learning. The building will gather together great intellectuals who will stimulate the development of knowledge."

"Sounds expensive to me," said Price. "How are you going to get these great intellectuals?"

"I think you will find that not all people are motivated by money," answered Pennington. "There are many who long for such a rarefied atmosphere, and there is already such a model for this idea at the Center for the Study of Democratic Institutions in Santa Barbara, California.[1]

"Sounds like a classic picture of Greek life," said Estabrook.

"We are seeking answers that are wise answers," replied Pennington. "We feel that wise men see things much more acutely than the man in the street."

"It sounds impractical to me," said Beattie. "Just more talk with little action."

Pennington stroked his chin reflectively and began again, "But don't all of you understand that education is not supposed to be practical in your narrow sense of that word? Was it practical for Socrates to spend all of his time trying to teach others? Was it practical of St. Thomas to devote his life to summing up religious thought?

---

[1]The Center for the Study of Democratic Institutions was set up under the direction of Robert M. Hutchins to bring together a number of thinkers for the purpose of studying contemporary problems.

I think we are too sold on the word 'practical' to do things that have much greater depth and importance."

"As I shall recall," said Reed, "the charge has already been made that you are developing an elitist program of education. Now that I hear you describe it, it sounds even more so."

"We feel that everyone profits more by dealing with things that have lasting value than those that are transitory," replied Pennington, "and we certainly do realize that some will go further than others in this direction. However, we react strongly against the idea that because some students cannot grasp great ideas as readily as others, that therefore they shouldn't deal with the great ideas at all, that they should be put to woodworking or something."

"This is very ethical," responded Reed, "but not too sound a policy in the light of where our schools are now. We would have to alter seriously our present mode of life to achieve what you have in mind."

"I think that is probably true," the perennialist replied. "We do feel that some of you, for whatever good intentions you may have had, promoted ideas in education that have led us, shall I say, downhill."

"Well, I must say that I do feel some affront," said Price, "to your slam against woodworking. Perhaps a student might not become involved with great ideas, but at least he would be learning something useful."

"It is not that we mind someone working with his hands," Pennington retorted, "but you asked me for a principle rather than an answer to a specific case. The principle of the thing would be that we would prefer that a person learn to think."

"Perhaps you might tell us how to develop such thought," replied Extan.

"Yes," said Pennington. "The great books were already mentioned. We feel that they are to be read not for mere amusement, as so many books are intended, but for the quality of ideas that exist there. It is for this reason that we feel most students need some help in learning how to handle such ideas, as well as in learning how to read such books with understanding. The dialectic, we feel, would be a very helpful tool, and very useful if brought back into the educational process. Basically, we feel that the development of the mind is quite important and that it should receive first priority."

Estabrook looked about the group and then straight at Pennington and said, "I must say that I am somewhat astounded to see what the perennialist proposes when it is laid out. It just sounds too otherworldly for me. Perhaps, if you gentlemen will allow, I'll develop my own ideas, and that will serve as an example of what I mean. First of all we are opposed to the kind of theorizing that Pennington seems to promote. We believe in research in education, and in developing creative people, and we do feel that this can be done by first making sure that the student knows the fund of knowledge that already exists. We would try to develop a program that would help the student know essential things, and then he can build other essential things on that. Ours is such a program. We know that such a fund of knowledge does exist, and we hope to present it to the student in terms of laws, principles, and so on, that he can apply to a wide variety of situations."

"How would you efficiently teach such things?" asked Beattie, leaning back in his chair.

"One way would be to utilize some of the research you have developed," replied the essentialist. "While we are somewhat aghast at what we feel is your mechanistic attitude toward man, we do feel that devices such as teaching machines and computers can be very effective in helping people to learn the important ideas of the universe. Though we recognize that all ideas have philosophical meaning to some extent, we think it is much better to use ideas than to continuously hash over their origin and development. For example, we know how to utilize electricity though we don't understand what it is. In the same way we can use knowledge for some purpose without really understanding what the nature of knowledge is."

"But how do you know you're using it correctly?" asked Pennington.

"We don't. Our role as teachers is to make sure that others know about things. Of course we are concerned with the morality of knowledge as the rest of you are, and hopefully some plan will eventually come out of putting together what we really know about the universe. For example, there are some elaborate steps now being taken by people like Buckminster Fuller[2] to put all of our existing knowledge into computers. When that is done we shall be able to synthesize our knowledge in such a way as to make it even more helpful to us."

"Helpful? In what way?" asked Extan.

"Helpful in the sense of developing a stronger economy, helpful in wresting further secrets from nature, helpful in creating new

---

[2]R. Buckminster Fuller is presently University Professor at Southern Illinois University, Carbondale, Illinois. He is well known as an engineer, architect, and designer. He is the author of numerous works, among which is *Utopia or Oblivion: the Prospect for Humanity* (New York: Bantam, 1969).

synthetics and minerals, helpful in a variety of ways to make man live better," replied Estabrook.

"I think one might say," said Pennington, "that we have been proceeding along your line for some time now, that the history of education has been largely along essentialist lines, and yet we are facing a world today where man's ability to do things has greatly outstripped his wisdom to use these things in the right way."

"There has always been war, poverty, and so on, but there is much less now than before. Despite what problems there are, things are better than they used to be. People eat better, wear better clothing, have better health care, and yes, they can defend themselves better than ever before. As to your statement that the schools have been run largely along 'essential' lines, I think that this is true up to a point. We feel, however, that there are certain trends today away from an essentialistic point of view, that this has already happened to some extent, and that it is a very dangerous trend."

"Could you specify what those forces might be?" questioned the reconstructionist.

"Yes," replied Estabrook. "Your influence, as well as that of the perennialist, has been slight in recent years, but we feel that progressivism, as well as existentialism, which have many adherents, are serving to undermine the traditional pattern of education."

"I'm certainly glad to hear that," replied Price. "We have always reacted negatively to the kind of data accumulation you essentialists have promoted from the time of the Puritans on. One of your problems, too, is that as one set of facts is learned it becomes very hard to switch to new ones. There is always a fact-gap, as it were. We are not opposed to facts per se, but we do resist the blind worship of them, whether they are religious facts or scientific ones."

"Although I have my own objections to progressivism," said Extan, "I am opposed to your philosophy of essentialism for what it has done to man. He has to a large extent been brutalized by the facts, just as he has been brutalized by philosophy. We like to think of man as more important than the facts, even though we recognize the importance of some facts needed in the process of man's survival. We are opposed to fact-getting as an end in itself, or as a way of preserving society as it is."

"It's very fashionable, it seems to me," said Estabrook, "to put essentialism down. And yet, we have done more for man than all the rest of you put together. We only hope we will be strong enough to survive you, and if we are not, then we feel that mankind will not survive either."

"The essentialist has delivered a rather passionate appeal for his case," volunteered Price. "Now, if you don't mind I should like to continue putting forward my own position. To begin with, we feel that learning a lot of data is a waste of time, and that this applies equally well to learning rules. We think it is much more efficient to develop individuals who can think creatively about a wide variety of issues. In today's world, particularly, where we don't know what kinds of problems we'll face, we need to be concerned that we are turning out people who can deal with problems effectively on any level. Due to the increasing number of people being relocated in the labor market we need to help people to learn new things quickly, and this can only be done well if they have been given some training in how to deal with problems. Thus, we would like to set up an educational program that would present meaningful problems and aid students in learning how to problem-solve."

"Yes, but what about the charge that progressivists are only concerned with present problems, with life adjustment?" queried Pennington. "I mean, couldn't one learn how to problem-solve as a way of fitting into society, even if that society were a bad one."

"Yes, that's true," said Price. "One might use problem-solving for that purpose. But we feel that problem-solving also leads to changes in society, that it promotes a constant search for new things to make life work better, and in that sense it is process rather than product."

"I think we've been over this ground before," said Reed, "but this whole idea of making 'life work better' seems to bother me. How do you know when something works? I mean, don't you have to have certain goals in mind to know whether something worked or not?"

"If it solved the problem then it worked," said Price. "We want a humanistic and peaceful society, but we feel that it can only come about through solving our day-to-day problems in a meaningful way."

"Yes," said Reed, "but we sort of feel that you're putting band-aids on the problems rather than solving them. For example, you feel that we can correct current situations and institutions by making them work better, whereas we feel that the institutions themselves might have to be changed. You are really blocking the road as far as we are concerned. And you are much more dangerous than the other philosophies because you are effective in keeping the archaic machinery of society going."

"That's a rather sweeping statement," the progressivist replied. "We have always been in the forefront of change. It is just that we see change taking place in an orderly fashion whereas you want it all done overnight, and that can not be done."

"The thing that bothers me about this term 'work' is that it is so nebulous," said Pennington. "What works in one case may not in another. What might work for one individual might not for another. It is like having a tool or instrument for moving ahead without any direction whatsoever. I do feel myself to be in agreement with the reconstructionist in that we need to have some goals in mind before using such an instrument."

"The goal is to change life for the better," said Price. "We are constantly improving everything. Everything can be made better, but not without change.

"The thing that is so important about change is that you must either be moving ahead or you are going backward. Change is involved in our very survival, and certainly in our improvement. Further, every person encounters problems or hurdles in life. We hope to help man get over those hurdles so he can lead a fuller and a richer life."

"If I might begin on that point," interrupted Reed, "this is why it is important to know where we are going first. We do need change, and I agree with the progressivist that we can only improve through change. However, I think we should be greatly concerned about the direction of our change. We can, I think, as the essentialist points out, go full steam ahead to oblivion. We have many scientists who are good problem-solvers, and yet may be providing solutions which will lead to our eventual extinction. Besides, without an adequate conception of goals we may be involved in solving minor rather than the major problems of society. We feel that education should lend itself to the reconstruction of human experience within a societal framework. We see a world in which spirit, facts, and problem-solving will all have a place, but it will be a world where, hopefully, man can have a freer, richer life."

"That's all very fine," said Estabrook, "but just how are you going to bring this about?"

"Yes, and how with particular reference to democratic procedures that you talk about so glibly?" questioned the progressivist.

"This is where education comes in," replied Reed. "We feel that education should be reconstructed in ways which will generate a desire for change. Unfortunately, our present system is too involved with maintaining the status quo, thus education becomes a supporting factor for many brutal and corrupting social forces. We would like to have people read more future-oriented works, and involve themselves in creative open-ended projects. You mentioned democracy. Yes, we are committed to a democratic approach. We feel that people should be made to see that certain changes are in their own best interest, and we feel that education has a role in bringing this about. We want man to have a vision of a better world, and having this vision he will then begin to reshape society in new ways."

"In many ways this is a very dangerous concept," said Price. "That is, by directing people's interests to these long range goals you may deflect their attention and efforts from solving more immediate and necessary problems."

"I've heard that charge many times," replied the reconstructionist. "But we have no intention of directing their interest from present problems. We just want them to see that their immediate problems may not really be solved until some attempt is made to solve them on a long-range basis."

"I can't help thinking, however," said Extan, "that you have some naïve notion that by changing society, whatever that means, you will somehow change man. If, for example, we were to create your shining utopia, and then place man in it as he presently exists, you would find that he would quickly change utopia to the same kind of world we live in today."

"That is probably true," admitted Reed, "and that is why we feel that education should also make some progress in changing man. It's a two-way street really. Society changes man and man changes society."

"Yes," said Extan, "but I still find it too pat for my taste. Where is a sense of tragedy, suffering, even trouble? Although most of the utopias I know of leave no room for such things, they exist. They always will exist."

"I'm not so sure about that," stated Reed. "It's true that we've always had suffering, tragedy, disease, to some extent, but I think it's very dangerous to feel that they must exist. We've made some improvement already, I feel, and we can go further. No, I don't think you can have an absolutely perfect society any more than you can have an absolutely perfect man, but we can do better."

"If I may pick up at this point," interjected Beattie, "I think perhaps many of you are not really aware of how far our technological revolution has already taken us. We do know that we can change human behavior in enormous ways, and that we can do this in ways that improve such behavior. All of your philosophies have effected little change in this respect, as is true with all religions, but now through the scientific control of behavior we can engineer people to be pretty much what we want them to be, which in turn will change society. The only thing that's really needed is your desire to put such a program into operation. Look at your schools. You are constantly trying to modify behavior but without real success. Your rewards are applied infrequently and with little consistency. Reinforcement is not maximized. But if we were to apply the discoveries of the behavioral sciences to education we could effect a great change in a very short period of time. I, personally, find the goals of the reconstructionist quite possible even in our own time, though I do think his methods are somewhat vague."

"But can the end, even if it is utopia, justify a method of controlling human behavior?" asked Pennington. "What about free will? What about democratic processes?"

"Free will is an illusion," replied Beattie. "As to democratic processes, democracy is a state of mind. If people believe they're free, or if they believe they are operating democratically, then for all intents and purposes they are. We can make people believe they're free."

"I must say that I share the perennialist's concern," said Extan. "When you destroy the right of people to choose, to commit themselves, you in effect destroy the individual. He then becomes a thing, a puppet."

"I must consider that a rather naïve remark," responded Beattie. "Everyone is controlled in one way or another already. We are all a product of our experiences, of our environment; actions that we believe are free are really actions that were determined in some way or other by our past experiences. We are all other-directed to some extent. It is just that for the first time we want to control the forces that act randomly upon people, and because they act randomly, do not really condition them in any complete sense. I would assume, however, that the decision to condition or not to condition would be arrived at democratically, at least to the extent that that is possible."

"Your view of man is somewhat belittling, I think," said Price. "Even though I have serious disagreements with the others here, I find your proposals the most inhumane of all."

"You shouldn't. You're interested in problem-solving. We can turn out problem-solvers by the dozen, or perennialists, existentialists, or what have you. You only have to make the decision as to what you want. However, we do find people unwilling to make any decision in this respect. Perhaps you call that inhumane. I don't."

"But there must be more to man than that," said Pennington. "You're just turning out automatons."

"Hardly," answered the behavioral engineer. "We can make people as human as you want. We can build in emotions, an aesthetic feeling, a religious fervor, all very human qualities, I believe."

"I find it rather frightening," said Pennington.

"Yes, it can be," replied Beattie. "But it is all within the range of possibility. The question is, will we undertake to engineer man's behavior toward all the good qualities, or will we leave it to others to use this power to condition him toward evil? There is an important and urgent decision to be made here."

"I propose that we don't condition him at all," said Extan.

"Yes, but that is impossible," Beattie retorted. "The only choice is who is to do it."

"If I may explain myself further," said the existentialist, "I do find what the behavioral engineer is suggesting a rather frightening prospect. But then, I find what all of you are suggesting also rather frightening. All of you want to manipulate man for some purpose of your own. The perennialist wants him to learn the great ideas; the essentialist, the facts; the progressivist wants problem-solving; the reconstructionist would like to create the new society; the behavioral engineer envisions making man into a machine. We want each individual to make the decision for himself as to what he will become, not you. When the decision is made for him, man becomes a non-person, inauthentic, artificial. Yes, perhaps you might make, at least in your terms, the best decision. But we would rather that man make the decision and that it be wrong, than for you to make it for him and it be right. All of you place your own ideas, your systems, higher than man. In effect, you destroy what is truly human about him. We would like to affirm the freedom of man. It is true that in today's world man is tossed about, manipulated, controlled, but we decry it. We want man to control himself, to take charge of his own destiny; to take charge whether it lead to disaster or glory."

"Yes, that is all fine talk," said Beattie, "but not very realistic. How many people do you know who are really independent, creative, controlling their own affairs? However, we could condition man to so act, to become self-reliant, and even authentic."

"I find that a contradiction in itself," said Extan. "You are in effect destroying that which is truly human about man, his right to make a decision, even a wrong decision. We know man's weaknesses, but we would rather he be man with all his shortcomings than your *Brave New World* person. We know, too, how man is already controlled by advertising, by education, by his society. We want to encourage people to become individuals who can understand the forces that attempt to control them and rise above them. We don't want uniformity, nor do we want individuals controlled for their own good. What we want are 'authentic' individuals—people who can act with convictions upon that which they have freely chosen; men who understand the forces that act to control and abate human freedom, and who work in ways that end such control."

"What you really want is anarchy," said Pennington. "I'm very familiar with the sloganeering of existentialism which says 'Do your own thing!' but that is nothing new in the history of thought, and a very dangerous concept besides. Man must learn to work within a system, to follow rules he may not immediately agree with for the sake of the whole."

"We don't believe that the whole is worth preserving at the expense of the individual," replied Extan. "Man is much more important than the system, no matter how good that system may be."

"You mentioned education as a detrimental factor in man's development," said Reed. "Perhaps you might comment on this a bit more."

"Yes," said the existentialist. "We feel that education as it presently exists only serves to make man fit the system, to become something: a doctor, a lawyer, an engineer, a part of the established pattern. We also think that the conditioning the behavioral engineer mentioned has always gone on in education, and that the whole process is one which subverts man's true nature. He is taught to accept, to follow conventions, rather than to be a free person. We want an educational program which promotes freedom and independence, not one which enslaves man and makes him a consumer, a technician, a false person."

"I think we all agree that man should be independent, creative and humane," said Estabrook, "but I really wonder if man would become that if all the restraints were removed. I think that history teaches us differently. I agree with the progressivist that we need to change our laws, even society, but I wonder if it can really be done by throwing aside all that has been developed during the past history of mankind."

"We are not asking man to throw it all aside," said Extan. "We are asking him to reexamine it, and particularly to reexamine it in the light of what it has done to him as a person. He may then disregard that part of history which does not contribute to his authenticity. I am sure that the perennialist would agree that we should know ourselves, and we feel that when individuals know themselves, they will make the kinds of choices that are best for them. We do not put a premium on whether any particular kind of society should exist, but we do feel that man should exist in the fullest sense of that term, and he can only do this as he begins to act like a person and to make commitments of his own. If you look at our present educational system, you will see that it rewards conformity, it rewards all the wrong things, and that man becomes manipulated by the system; he becomes a thing, rather than a person. He lives, but as we use the term, he does not *exist*."

"Gentlemen," said Price. "I find all of this very interesting, but I sometimes think we stray quite a bit from the topic at hand. What I should like to ask the existentialist, as I would like all of you to keep in mind, is what should we do with education specifically?"

"I shall put it this way," began the existentialist. "Imagine an art class where the teacher brings a bowl of fruit into the room and asks the students to paint it. Some of the students begin by painting the fruit surrealistically, some are doing abstract fruit, others pointillism, and there is even an aspiring Jackson Pollock in the class. The teacher looks over all the paintings, but the ones she commends the highest are those that are done realistically because she personally likes realism, so that the next time art class meets everyone does things realistically. Now, what has this teacher done? She has forced her values upon the class. She has stifled natural creativity. She likes realism, and therefore they must like it."

"She was conditioning them," said Beattie.

"This is true," admitted Extan, "and it is a type of conditioning we are against. We find this sort of thing going on not only in art but in every area of the curriculum; in history where the teacher stresses certain events or personages over others, in geography where some countries receive more attention than they deserve, and in every other area as well."

"I share the existentialist's concern in this respect," said Reed. "There is quite too much brainwashing in education, but what I would like to know at this point is what each of you recommends for change in American education? You've pretty much said what you are against. But what are you for?"

"If you would like me to continue on that," said Extan, "I would be happy to do so. We are for an end to authoritarianism in education with more freedom of choice within the educational process. We think that all students should have a say in the kind of education they want, if not the total say, and we feel that education should become much more individualized than it is at present."

"If I may interrupt here for a moment," said the progressivist, "we have been stressing those things for years. You are relatively new to education, and you state these points as if you are the only one who believes them."

"We know what you stand for," said Extan, "and we feel that progressivism has greatly improved the condition of education, but we also feel that now is a time to go further. I rather doubt that you are as yet ready to go to the extremes we feel are necessary to change education. For example, you talk about the teacher as a guide rather than an authoritarian ruler. We feel that being a guide is still a manipulator of sorts, and that such things as a 'guide,' or 'controlled freedom' which the Montessori people promote, is still too much manipulation of the student. You are still thinking of students as 'Its' rather than 'Thous'; and what I mean by Thou is treating the individual as a person rather than as an object, i.e., an It. The student is someone who makes a choice because you have set up the situation to make him make that choice. You use his interests, his background, and all the rest to cause him to choose something that you think is good for him. We feel that the student should be totally free, or as free as possible, and encouraged to make his own free choices as to what he wants. We really don't care whether he goes to school or not. What is important is that he is doing what he wants to do."

"But suppose," said Estabrook, "that one chooses not to go to school or to study history, or mathematics. What will happen to society?"

"Is society more important than man? Why should man be made to do something that is not good for him but may be good for some abstraction, such as society? We feel this is a misplaced emphasis."

"I shudder to think what would happen if this were promoted on a wide scale," said Estabrook.

"Actually, the result is not so frightening as you make it out to be," replied Extan. "We find that when students are left free to make their own choices that they usually make better ones than when those choices are made for them."

"If I might interject again," said Price, "we have constantly stated that children have a natural curiosity about the world, and that unfortunately much of what passes for education tends to stifle that natural curiosity."

"Yes, I think that is true," replied Extan. "But what we want are people who do things because they want to rather than because they are told they have to, or because it will gain them a certain income, or help them to arrive at certain social advantages."

"But don't such students often make wrong choices?" asked Pennington.

"Yes, they sometimes do," said Extan. "But it is their choice and they have to live with it."

"The idea of making such important choices is rather serious business," said Estabrook. "One could ruin one's life by not making the right choices."

"Yet," said Extan, "there are many who probably made the right choices in your sense of the term and became doctors, lawyers, and engineers, only to discover that their lives were meaningless, unhappy, and completely other-directed. We really don't care what people become except as it is their choice to become so."

"Yes, I read *Summerhill*,"[3] said Estabrook. "Is that what you're promoting?"

"There are many existentialists who feel that *Summerhill* does offer a kind of attitude about education that we think it fruitful to explore. However, I think that some criticism might be made of Neill who in many ways resembles the Frazier of *Walden Two*[4] and manipulates people toward becoming such and such. We do feel that Summerhill is a vast improvement over current practice, however."

"I think," said Reed, "that if we hope to develop this dialogue in terms of our best ideas that it would be profitable to keep each session fairly short and then meet informally between sessions to discuss and go over some of the things that have already been stated."

"Yes, I agree," replied Price. "I think we need to have some time to mull over the ideas that have already been put forth."

The six philosophers agreed with this suggestion and decided to meet again the next day at the same time to continue the discussion from the point where it had terminated.

---

[3] *Summerhill* was written by A. S. Neill (N.Y.: Hart Publishing Co., 1960). It is a private school in Leiston, England, which professes a radical approach to child-rearing where children are not under the restraints of ordinary schools. Van Cleve Morris (*Existentialism in Education,* N.Y.: Harper and Row, 1966) discusses Summerhill as a school that is primarily existential in nature. See pp. 147–150.

[4] *Walden Two* by B. F. Skinner (N.Y. The Macmillan Co., 1948) is a utopian treatise dealing with a society based on the principle of behavioral engineering. Frazier is the founder and directing force of Walden Two.

Questions for Discussion

1. Do you think that EDCO's project to examine educational philosophy as a first step in making proposals for education is a valid one? Do you agree with the statement made by the EDCO representative that everything is eclectic in some way?

2. Why does it take the educational philosophers so long to get started in this discussion? Is there any value in their delay? Do you agree with the approach they agreed upon?

3. How would you respond to Reed's point (p. 5) that Nazis were good problem solvers? What is his intent in making such a statement?

4. How would you analyze Pennington's statement (p. 7) that "We don't know what the future will bring, but we do know what the past has been."?

5. Do you agree with Price that the word "spiritual" implies a certain occult influence? (p. 11)

6. Do you agree with Pennington's philosophical views? Why or why not?

7. Does the term "work" as viewed by the progressivist bother you as much as it does Reed and Pennington? (p. 17)

8. Do you agree with Extan's view that Neill (*Summerhill*) resembles Frazier of *Walden Two?* (p. 25)

9. What is your overall response to the discussion at this point? What philosopher do you think presented the strongest argument? Why?

2

The Second Day

The meeting convened on the second day without Edwards being present. Our educational philosophers, now refreshed with food and sleep, looked forward to another day of debate. They all realized that the previous day's discussion had left a lot of loose ends, that many of the issues needed a great deal more clarification. They eagerly looked forward to finishing yesterday's business as well as raising new issues.

Estabrook, who had had great difficulty containing himself at the close of the last meeting when Extan maintained his feeling that *Summerhill* was a vast improvement over current practice in education, was the first to speak.

"I must say at this point, gentlemen," he began, "that not only am I opposed to the philosophy which underlies *Summerhill*, but I even feel that many of our present problems in education, and with young people in general, are a direct consequence of such a philosophy. Whatever happened to the idea of discipline? I am sure that everyone here had to take courses they didn't like, only to find out later how valuable they were. Let me then, if I may, state what I think is the kind of program we should have. I think I have intimated what I would like already, but now, I hope to be much more specific. First of all, we feel that there is some basic subject matter that everyone should know. I would like to think that everyone here would be in agreement that it is very desirable to have children know how to read, to write, and to do arithmetic. Also, I think we could add other valuable subjects such as science, history, and perhaps foreign languages, as very vital and basic subject matter in today's world. We feel, like the progressivist, that such subject matter should be presented in the most interesting way possible. However, we do not think that just because a student is not interested in it that it should not be taught, or because he is more interested in something else, such as tiger hunting, that that should be used to replace more basic subject matter. We also feel that such subjects should be taught early and continued in more complex fashion throughout the life of an individual. For example, a student would start with simple arithmetic, then go on to algebra, geometry, and calculus. We realize that not every individual can be proficient in all of these subjects, but we feel that we have an obligation to present them to him in as interesting a manner as possible and to take him as far as he can go. Because he doesn't like it, or even because he can't do it, is no reason for not exposing him to it. We feel very strongly that basic skills are not only important for the individual, but for the very preservation of culture. A nation that falls behind in basic skills becomes a prey for other stronger nations. We need to keep our country strong, and we can only do this when we keep our educational skills up to a very high level."

"What about subjects like philosophy, poetry, and art? Where would they fit in your curriculum?" asked Pennington.

"We feel that such areas are important," replied the essentialist. "Hopefully, they will be integrated with other areas. But in terms of importance they are not as important as the other basic areas I mentioned."

"I seem to detect in all that you are saying," said Reed, "very definite political overtones. Are you not in effect saying that you feel that essentialism is a desirable educational philosophy because it will tend to preserve the kinds of values we have at the present time?"

"I don't know what you mean by preserve. However, if you mean that there are some basic values that need to be maintained, I suppose I would say that that is true. I want you to understand that we do not feel that values shouldn't change, such as the position the perennialist promotes, nor do we accept the constant change of the progressivist and the reconstructionist; we feel that we should stick to our present values until we find something better to take their place. Our view is that man has steadily been accumulating useful knowledge. Let us say that as a caveman he knew how to make a spear. This knowledge was very important and needed to be taught to others, to his children, for example. Today, we do not feel that spearmaking deserves a place in the curriculum for there are other more important things to know, such as mathematics, for example. We are upset, however, at the number of really important areas that are neglected or shunted aside for courses we feel are irrelevant to man's needs in our twentieth century culture."

"I would like to ask the essentialist this," said Beattie. "If we take your position that these essential, basically fact-type courses are what we should offer in the schools—history, mathematics, etc.—isn't it true that machines could probably do a better job of teaching them than people?"

"Well, at the present time we do not feel that our technology is that far advanced," said Estabrook. "However, it is very likely that this will happen at some point. We find programmed learning very commendable. The programs are frequently better thought out than a program presented by the average teacher, and we find a high degree of motivation and retention. We are not really worried about the educator being out of a job—at least not at this point. But what's the purpose of education anyway? Just to get people jobs? If machines can do the job better, then machines should be used."

"What about things like creativity?" queried Pennington. "Would you have a place for that?"

"As with poetry and the fine arts, we think creativity is very useful. We really feel that one should deal with any kind of material creatively, but if you mean for leisure activity, as a hobby, I think that such courses might be taught, but only as an adjunct to the higher priority courses I mentioned. We are quite disturbed by the so-called appreciation or survey courses. We feel that these courses are not really education in the true sense of the term. It reminds me of that line from Pope that a little learning is a dangerous thing. We're for education in depth in essential areas, and there is only so much time. We think that things like driver education, social awareness, creative dancing and all the rest, if they are to be taught at all, should be taught outside of the regular academic program."

"Students want such courses as driver education, sex education, and all the rest," said Price.

"I know they do," answered Estabrook. "But just because someone wants something does not mean they should get it. There are some students who will select a tough academic program, but there are many others who will take the easy way out if you let them."

"If you don't mind, gentlemen," said Price, "I shall begin my response by pursuing this statement made by the essentialist about education in depth. First of all, the phrase is quite an *ad populum* term. Who is opposed to education in depth? No one. Indeed, it is somewhat like motherhood. The question is, what does education in depth mean in practice? What is it in terms of essentialist teaching? To begin with, we find that what education in depth means in practice is memorization, rote learning, facts, dates, battles, and all the rest of those things that one seldom is called upon to use. Most students hate the method even though some of them become good at it. But does it really achieve education in depth? I say it does not. I think that the perennialist is much more an educator in depth than the essentialist. This is to say that if one really wanted to understand things in depth, instead of learning the dates, names, and battles, he would examine the philosophy of war, the meaning of brotherhood, and that which underlies the events of history. I do not think that studying history, particularly from the viewpoint of an essentialist, will give you education in depth. It is a very superficial view of what history is all about. As to the facts learned, one always finds some facts that are important, but we usually forget most of them, or we find that they are wrong, or that they are out of date. Even the essentialist would admit that facts change, such as the 'fact' prior to our nuclear age that the atom could not be split, or the 'fact' that the earth was a sphere before we found that it bulged out at the sides and looks more pear-shaped than spherical. We are not opposed to facts, but we find that facts and other data can be learned in connection with activities that are interesting and useful. Our emphasis is not on facts as facts, but facts as a resource you can do something with. We are much more interested in facts as methods than as ends. Most lawyers do not know all of the cases that have been heard in American jurisprudence, but they do know where to find them when they need them. I grant you that it might be nice to have them all committed to memory, but it is unnecessary if one knows how to find them when needed."

"What you are doing," said Estabrook, "is setting up a straw man. I am not for learning facts just to learn facts either. They are to be useful. Nor does the learning of facts have to be dull. Some people find it very interesting. Nor are we opposed to problem-solving. As in your case with the lawyer, we don't think he should memorize all the cases either, but on the other hand we think he should have some basic knowledge about the law inside him. He is not just a blank mind that grabs a book off a shelf for every single question he is asked."

"You also railed against appreciation courses," said Price. "We are not against students going into these in great depth, and many do. What we are attempting to do is to give them a taste, and hopefully to present them in ways that encourage them to study further. If one were to teach music as an essentialist would, he might begin with notes and chord structure. Most students find this boring and do not pursue music from that point on, unless they are forced to, as many are. We feel that music should be presented in ways that make students want to know more about it, and perhaps to become musicians themselves. We do not pretend that survey courses and appreciation courses are ends in themselves. They are a means to an end, and that is to develop as fully as possible whatever potential the student has for music or anything else."

"Yes," replied Estabrook, "so that theoretically one might decide to continue in-depth programs in basket weaving or driver education or cooking."

"Well, what's wrong with that?" replied the progressivist. "Do you think that everyone should be a scientist? Isn't there any room in society for basket weavers?"

"Yes, of course," said Estabrook. "And there should be. Only we find students who can do higher things are doing basket weaving. We don't really feel that that is developing the potential of a student to the fullest."

"You know," said Price, "all your talk about the school is like talk about some little island where only so much is supposed to go on. We see the school in much larger terms. We see the school as a place of germination where the student is encouraged to pursue things on the outside. And if he likes them he will. Utilizing your approach, however, makes students think of studies as punishment and therefore they don't study when they don't have to."

"I believe the original question was: What steps would you take to improve education?" said Beattie.

"To begin with," said Price, "it is not surprising that the essentialist and I would have differences, for although I feel that the schools have gone a good way in the progressivist direction I still feel that there is still too much of the essentialist orientation in education, particularly at the high school and college level. The essentialist likes to divide things into neat little categories, whereas we would like to see more of the subjects unified. This has happened somewhat already: Subjects such as reading, writing, and other communication skills have been placed under a category known as language arts; and subjects like history, geography, and sociology are designated as social studies. We feel that the school should go further in this direction and show the relationship that exists between language arts and social studies, as well as between all other subjects in the curriculum. When one goes to a cocktail party he doesn't find one group discussing only history, another art, and still another philosophy. They are really discussing matters that touch on a variety of curriculum areas, and the intelligent man knows how to apply what he has learned to the particular problems under discussion. We think that the rigid classification of courses that now exists should be done away with, and that educators should work together to integrate their special skills into a meaningful whole. We would like to see learning done more in terms of strategies, i.e., strategies for attacking particular problems. We do not feel that learning is an end in itself. It is something one uses, and we feel it has a very special use in solving problems. We want to see the schools become more open and democratic. There is still too much lock-step work. We would like to see students pursuing things they are interested in, and we would like to do away with as many taboos as possible about what a student should or should not study. We want to see students take a greater role in shaping the structure of what they learn, as well as the area in which learning takes place. We would like to create intelligent teachers who know how to guide a student's learning without becoming autocratic and cruel. We would also like to see the schools become more naturalistic and humanistic. We want them to reflect the natural development of individuals, and we want them to help people develop values that make them treat other people fairly while they are in the process of becoming productive human beings."

"This idea of a teacher as a guide disturbs me somewhat," said Extan. "Why should anyone be guided? You rail against the perennialist and the essentialist for directing education in a specific way, and yet you do it yourself, perhaps more subtly, but you are still doing it."

"I think that the difference," answered Price, "is one between force and suggestion. We do not say that a student must do this and that. We only try to encourage him to do this and that. For example, we feel that mathematics is important and we try various ways of getting him interested in mathematics."

"But suppose you couldn't find a way?" asked the existentialist.

"We think there is always a way," stated Price.

"I must say that what you have said here certainly shows no promise of helping the student to change things," added Reed. "Based on what you've said, the life-adjustment charge seems to have some validity."

"We are not really creating revolutionaries," said Price. "We think that there should be constant change, but in an orderly systematic way."

"All of this talk about student interest sounds nice," said Pennington, and the freedom and all that, but I've found that when you arrange a school along your lines that bedlam breaks loose."

"There probably is a bit more hustle and bustle, and noise," said Price, "but we don't place that high a value on silence. Just because a classroom is quiet does not mean that worthwhile things are going on. They just may be in fear of the teacher."

"I'd like to say a few words about progressivism as a way of getting into perennialism," said Pennington. "It is true that we would have some serious differences regarding discipline and subject matter and so on, but the major difference is one you avoided mentioning altogether. Progressivism does encourage teaching children how to fend for themselves and even how to become successful at it, but it neglects a very important need and that is the development of the other side of man, the spiritual side. The behavioral engineer seems to treat man as a lot of wires and test tubes, and though you don't do that, you do seem to treat him as only blood, muscle, and brain matter. We feel there is something more, not just the human but the divine side of man. Now, it has been asked what steps we would take to improve education. I would take the following: To begin with, there should be better kinds of material to read. Instead of reading Dick and Jane and other mass produced literature, children should be reading great literature. If there is none available then we should have our best authors trying to produce some by writing especially for the schools. We should also encourage a great deal of thought, not only about day-to-day problems, but about the great ideas. We need to integrate things like philosophy and poetry on every level of schooling, and to try to give children and adults some feeling for greatness. We also feel that we need teachers who are not only trained technically, but are people who can serve as models, such as Socrates served for Plato. Basically, we do not see the schools primarily as a place for technicians or problem-solvers. Life is much more than that. The trouble with the world now is that there are too many people running around doing things without knowing why they are doing them. We need more thought and less action."

"Not only does your philosophy lend itself to inaction," said Price, "but it also leads to retarding developments in science and other fields."

"I think that if we were honest with ourselves," said the perennialist, "we would want some curb on technological development. We are proceeding faster in developing technology than learning to use it in the right way. We need to stop and reassess where we are, and our philosophy preaches just such self-awareness. We feel the concept 'know thyself' is just as valid today as it ever was."

"We existentialists would support your criticism of technology, and certainly support the 'know thyself' dictum," said Extan, "but what we are afraid of is what you do to the person in trying to foist your ready-made ideas upon him. You say you want him to think, but I rather think you want him to accept."

"We do feel, of course, that it is important to know the great ideas of the past, but we do not think he must accept any or all of them. Our Great Books approach belies your statement because you will see that there is a whole range of ideas there. The *Bible* is one of the great books, but so is *Das Kapital.* We don't say that they have to accept the ideas of either one, but we do think it important that they know about them."

"How about more modern authors and books?" asked Estabrook. "Don't you make provision for them?"

"As a matter of fact we do," said Pennington. "But we don't feel that it is beneficial for people to try to keep up with the best sellers. Usually they fade away in a few years. We would like people to read books that will probably have a long-range impact in terms of ideas. This is why we feel it is important to have some interpretation about what are good versus bad books."

"That's what I mean," said Extan. "You're always deciding what's good and what isn't. Isn't it just possible that a book which you might not think is good could serve a very valuable purpose with someone else?"

"Yes, that's true. We do feel that there are different intellectual levels, and that some people need to be listened to more than others. We aren't after thought control. We want to learn, and if we find someone who knows a great deal, whether he is ancient or modern, we pay attention to him."

"Your method seems to be quite bookish," said Price.

"Probably more than the rest of you," replied Pennington. "However, we do see value in nature studies, as well as the use of the dialectic as a learning tool. We feel that books contain a great deal of wisdom, but we think there is a certain wisdom in nature too. We are not quite so narrow as you suppose."

"How would you respond to the charge," said Beattie, "that there is a great religious emphasis in your approach, and that this can be seen in the fact that most parochial schools use a perennialist approach?"

"That's a rather complex question," replied Pennington. "To begin with there are a number of religious writings that we think people should read, but there are also anti-religious ones. We read *Candide, The Decline and Fall of the Roman Empire,* and so on. If you mean that religion stresses the search for wisdom and truth, I suppose that you could draw a connection there. It is true that this is usually stressed in a parochial educational program. We think you are correct in saying that although parochial education may be in part pragmatic, existential, and all the rest, its primary focus would be perennial. We decry the fact that so many secular college students take no courses in philosophy, but only in the more technical areas. About the only colleges that do officially stress philosophy are religious ones. We are not always in accord with the kind of philosophy stressed, but we do approve of the idea that there should be a philosophical orientation throughout one's schooling."

"One of the things that bothers me about these so-called great ideas," said Estabrook, "even admitting the fact that it seems like some kind of academic game, is that you get involved in an activity that may be very interesting and all that, but you never come out with anything you can use or that you can really say is dependable. Why should we have a student wasting his time studying philosophy in which one answer may be as good as another, when he could be learning chemistry or mathematics, or biology?"

"All we are asking," replied the perennialist, "is that people be taught from a philosophical point of view. We think that a student should be encouraged to know the whys of life as well as the hows. We feel that most subjects are taught as technical know-how courses rather than as methods to use in analyzing man and nature. Now, if you want to do both, that's fine. But we feel that the philosophical side should not be neglected, as we feel that it is in most of contemporary education. If someone can tell us how we can put the two together, we would be very grateful."

"I have never considered it that much of a problem," said Beattie. "It is unfortunate that we behavioral engineers have had such a hard time in making people believe that we are not just interested in the mechanical side of man. We can turn out philosophers too, as I believe I already mentioned at one point. I personally feel that philosophy is important, that people should have some concept of depth in what they do, and that this should be a part of their education. Let me try to develop this further. We have arrived at certain techniques which we can utilize in many different ways. I would not like to see us turn out only philosophers. I think we need doers too. But, assuming that we do think philosophy is important, as I think it is, then we can arrange an educational program that will turn out the desired kind of interest in philosophy. The reason why people are not interested in it now is due to some kind of aversive influence they encountered in their past education. If we can reinforce a more positive attitude toward philosophy, we can turn out philosophers by the bucketful."

"Programmed philosophers is a contradiction in terms," replied Pennington. "The nature of the philosopher is that he would be critical, even critical of the influences that led him to be a philosopher."

"Do you think that we are going to neglect criticism?" answered the behavioral engineer. "We can make your philosopher as critical as you want. We can also make him open-minded and tolerant, and I think you will agree that these are qualities that not too many philosophers have in real life."

"Just how would you program open-mindedness?" asked Extan.

"What we would do," said Beattie, "would be to set up situations where a student was reinforced only when he took all points of view into account. If, either because of haste or laziness, he would only consider a few points of view, he would not be rewarded. Unfortunately, in our present society, people are rewarded for making sweeping generalizations or because they present a very narrow interpretation of an issue. Let us say that we had some political issue. If a student only examined what one nation had to say about it, he would not be reinforced. He would have to search through a whole body of conflicting data and then make his mind up after that. I do not wish to give the impression that we think our purpose is only to turn out philosophers, critical or otherwise. But we do feel that a philosophical approach to society is useful, and we can develop it in people to the extent that it is necessary."

"Who is going to decide if it is necessary, and to what extent?" asked Reed.

"Yes, that's the hard question," replied Beattie. "We feel that since it is being done at the present time anyway, that people are being conditioned, someone must take the responsibility for using conditioning more effectively in order to turn out better people. I would hope that society could arrive at a consensus on certain goals we might use in shaping people better, perhaps the educators . . ."

"Let us say, just for the sake of argument," said Extan, "that you could turn out any kind of person you wanted to. What kind of person would you turn out?"

"I cannot speak for all behavioral engineers," said Beattie, "but if you are asking me personally, I would say this. My prototype of the ideal man would be one who had some of all the qualities you gentlemen are stressing. He would be a good problem-solver, he would know some technical facts, he would be philosophically oriented, and in addition, an individual. I might also add that he would have both aesthetic and humanistic impulses."

"That sounds like quite a package," said Pennington. "Is this for everyone or only a few?"

"Everyone, give or take a few," said Beattie. "The methods that we have are applicable across the board."

"How long would it take to develop this in American education?" asked Price.

"We could begin tomorrow," answered the behavioral engineer, "if most people were ready for our ideas, emotionally ready that is."

"I am sure they are not," said Estabrook.

"Yes, our ideas are yet to come," said Beattie. "That is why we have been more or less limited to making practical suggestions in order to move education slowly in this direction."

"What kinds of suggestions?" queried Estabrook.

"Well, first of all, many educators have been using conditioning for years without really realizing that they were conditioning. We are making them aware of what they are doing so that now they can do it more effectively. Also, the method of reinforcement has been slowly but steadily improving. Educators must learn to reward more consistently and immediately. They are coming to see the value of our ideas more and more. There are many rewards they can use: tokens, praise, food, or programmed learning in general—sometimes even success itself. Further, all of the advances being made in teaching machines, which are just beginning to make serious inroads in education, are all based on principles that we have developed."

"What do you really see happening in the next ten years?" asked Reed.

"I am not sure about ten or twenty, but I do see a very computerized educational system ahead. I see machines utilizing the principles of conditioning, as well as other mechanized devices finding their way into the schools. I also see teachers being trained in methods of conditioning, and I think we will begin to see greater agreement on what the aims of education should be so that we can begin to condition more effectively. I feel that time is on our side, and in the end you will see behavioral engineering the major aspect of all educational programs. But I would be very interested to hear what you as a reconstructionist think of all this. You've been trying to look into the future for some time. What do you see?"

"I agree with the use of conditioning," replied Reed, "and with the kinds of computerization and technology you mentioned. If anything, I see more of it than you do. When I look into the future, as you asked me to, what I see for American education is this. I think that every student, from perhaps kindergarten on, will have his own little cubicle. This may be in a school building or it may be at home. He will sit in that cubicle and be surrounded by all kinds of electronic gadgetry. He will have earphones so that he can hear tapes and records. There will be a screen so that at the press of a button he can get pictures and films regarding any area that interests him. He will have a typewriter where he can type questions on any subject and receive answers back immediately from a centralized information bank. To a certain extent he will be an engineer and his own boss. All of this is of course based on things that seem quite practical at the moment. Who knows what further ways of presenting knowledge will be discovered in the future, such as the possibilities of chemical learning, that can also be applied to the learning situation?"

"I wonder," said Price, "what this might do to childhood. I mean, the child is like a computer engineer going to work. I'm sure that he could be quite absorbed in his activities, but it seems to me that you aren't leaving any room for humor or for free play or all the rest of the things we usually associate with childhood."

"I suppose that is the picture I seemed to represent, but not what I intended," said Reed. "I feel that the time spent in the cubicle will be used so efficiently, that the child will learn so well, that he will have more free time than ever before. Certainly, I don't think we can neglect that side of a person's life. Also, I think we will see more kinds of learning activities developed in the home itself. TV will become more and more an educational medium, and every home in the future will have a few teaching machines."

"I am not sure that kind of world is one I would want to live in," said Pennington, "or the kind of education I would want for children."

"But why not?" asked the reconstructionist. "Nothing will be left out. The child will be happy and well adjusted. Compare it with the chaotic conditions you find in most schools today where children are bored, unhappy, and where education is associated with pain instead of pleasure."

"There is one thing that I feel needs to be mentioned," said Beattie. "I think that both of us talked about the changes of education, but wouldn't there have to be other changes, societal changes, in order to enable such educational changes to come about?"

"Yes, certainly," said Reed. "I think there would have to be sweeping changes throughout society in order to implement this kind of program. It might demand a change of government, or our attitude toward education and toward people in general. We need to have a commission that is studying futuristic ideas, but at the present time we don't have it."

"It does bother me somewhat that your future is always portrayed as more glowing and good than the present," said Pennington. "Why must we always be going somewhere? Isn't there some value to staying where one is?"

"No, I don't think so," answered Reed. "You either go ahead or you go backward. You can't stay where you are. Besides, we want people to use their minds, and to use them creatively. Things can always be made better, and we want people to take a part in making them better. Of course there is much more to it. A lot of things in our society need to be changed. We should start thinking about it. I don't think that real changes in education will come about without changes in society, and that is why we must interest ourselves in making societal changes as well as educational ones."

"How do you go about doing this?" asked Extan.

"We feel that educators must begin to take a more positive role in shaping the future. Traditionally, educators have always been the victims of change. They had to adapt to what came about. We feel that as intelligent responsible members of society they have a greater responsibility than most to see to it that people are educated in ways that lead toward their own self development as well as toward the further development of society. We would encourage teachers to become involved in social action causes. We would encourage students to do the same. What we want is more activism in education, and a dedication to something beyond the here and now, the status quo. We have been encouraged by the number of educators and students who have begun to move in this direction, and things like the Peace Corps, VISTA, and the rest are very reassuring to us, if only they could be administered more ably."

"How about basic subject matter?" questioned Estabrook. "How would you handle that?"

"We see the value of it, but not in and of itself," said Reed. "We feel it should be utilized in ways that promote change and the building of a new social order."

"Isn't it true that your philosophy disturbs many people," said Price, "because they are afraid of terms like 'the changing of the social order'? I mean some people feel you are going to dump democracy and all the other values they hold dear."

"We have constantly fought for democratic principles," answered the reconstructionist, "but we do not feel that a particular kind of government will be the government of the future just because it worked in some past time. I think that you would agree that a government should always be workable, only I suppose we are more honest than you in our implication that a more workable government could lead to a change of governments, even a rejection of democracy. There will always be a number of people who are frightened at such ideas because they are insecure about change. Usually, people don't want change if they are satisfied, but in our present society we find that they are often satisfied at the expense of someone else. With regard to capitalism, for example, there are a number of people who are always calling for laissez-faire, but what they really mean is that they don't want you to change something that is allowing them to exploit other people. We think people have to be open-ended about change. We also think there should be constant experimentation with the implementation of new ideas when they work, even ideas pertaining to economics and politics."

"Then you feel that schools should primarily be agents for change?" asked Extan.

"Yes. We feel that everything should be geared in this direction."

"And the educator rewards his students to the degree in which they are change agents?" asked Beattie.

"Yes," said Reed. "So long as the changes are constructive and not destructive. We believe in humanism, not change for change's sake, but changes that add to man's stature and growth."

"There has been quite a plea for humanism on the part of all of you," said Estabrook, "and I suppose no one would admit to being inhumane, and perhaps none of you are, but something that keeps cropping up as a question in my mind is your feeling toward man— I mean toward him basically. Is he good, evil, neutral, or what?"

"That's a very complex question," replied Pennington. "Very complex indeed. But a good one. I think that you might even say that the answer to that question determines to quite an extent the kind of educational programs we actually propose. For example, I would say that although we don't think of man as evil in the biblical sense of that term, though I will admit some do, that is, with sin, original or otherwise. Yet we do feel that man is weak and needs some help and direction. We don't think that man is born with any instinctive desire for knowledge, or to read the classics, or anything else. Although he has some of the angel in him, he is mostly animal at first. It is only with careful attention that he is directed to higher things. So that I would say, in your terms at least, that we do not think that man has any instinctive desire for the good as Rousseau proposes. We think that man can reach the good, but only with the proper guidance. Therefore, we must have some controls in our educational program. We don't think that one study is as good as another, that it doesn't matter what you choose, or that you can choose nothing if you want to. We think some things are better than others, that some things have a higher importance than others. Consequently, our program might be one of 'controlled freedom' or 'direction.'"

"I kind of wonder what 'controlled freedom' means," said Price. "You are either free or you aren't. What you're talking about sounds like a contradiction in terms."

"We don't think so. We know of no school system that promotes total freedom, i.e., anarchy. Everyone has rules and limits, whether they are set by educators or by students. We do tend to feel that although rules may be set by students, and that students should have some role in setting them, we still think that an older, more experienced person would generally be more adept in setting good and just rules, and that if he has the proper respect of his students they will obey them."

"Although you are unwilling to admit it," said Beattie, "I think that deep down you feel that man is evil. I know that all the classics don't promote that idea, but many do, perhaps even most. I mean if we look at it the other way around, isn't your desire for control and direction really a way of saying that you don't trust people to make the right decisions and that you need someone there to make sure they do? You mentioned before that many religions take a perennial approach toward education, and isn't the idea of evil very prevalent in religious philosophy? I mean look at the Puritans for example. They believed man to be evil and took a very perennial approach toward education. This explains why they believed so strongly in direction and corporal punishment and other restrictive and repressive measures. I personally feel that much of what is still repressive in education is a result of this perennial and religious viewpoint."

"I think you are damning me by association," said Pennington. "I agree that the Puritans had a perennial attitude toward education, and that they did indeed promote many harsh educational methods. But this is by no means true of perennialism today. We believe in some control, as I say all of you do, but we are also humanists, as indeed Maritain, who is a leading author of perennial educational philosophy, well shows."[1]

"I think the matter is a relative one," said Price. "All of us believe in rules to some extent. It is a matter of who makes the rules and how strong the rules are. In relation to progressivist philosophy I think we would have to say that you are more direction-oriented than we are."

"I must say that I do not find the perennialist's ideas about control too out of keeping with my own," said the essentialist. "We do not believe that man is capable of finding his own path, particularly during childhood. We think that man needs some sort of guidance for his own good. I don't think you can really tie me in with the Puritans, though perhaps you might try, but we feel that man is not born with the innate wisdom to know which is the best path to take. We do not like strong-arm measures, but we think that parents and educators should see to it that children learn the kinds of things that will be of great value to them later, though they might not see that value at the present time."

"It is true that you might not tie in well with the Puritans," said Extan. "But I would certainly tie you in with the kind of education that was prevalent in America from the middle half of the 1800s to the early 1900s. I think we are all familiar with that kind of education, which was like castor oil stuffed down the throats of children. It is the kind of education that Dickens so detested in his caricature of Mr. Grandgrind, and it is the kind of repressive education we connect with the story of Tom Sawyer."

"Yet we turned out many great men," stated Estabrook. "We don't think that education has to be distasteful. But we find it is hard to make really important things fun all the time."

"But do you feel that man is basically evil?" asked Reed.

"Again, I reply as did the perennialist: The word needs defining. We do not think that man will always choose what is in his best interest. We think that he often needs encouragement in that direction."

"Or needs to be forced in that direction?" asked Beattie.

"Gentle force," said Estabrook. "We think highly of man and of what he can do. It is because we think so highly of him that we don't want to see him waste himself or his talents. We know that civiliza-

---

[1]Jacques Maritain is the author of a number of works relating Christianity to education, principal among which is *Education at the Crossroads* (New Haven, Conn: Yale University Press, 1943). As a neo-Thomist, Maritain feels that the best education leads one to God.

tion contains rules. Without rules there is no civilization and consequently no order. Look at what happens in Golding's *Lord of the Flies*[2] when civilization is removed."

"I really do believe that the idea of looking at one's basic attitude toward man does reveal quite a bit about one's educational theories and practices," said Price. "Indeed, I found what both the perennialist and the essentialist had to say most fascinating, though I must say that I was not surprised at their responses. As for us, we have for years been reacting to just such an attitude as they express. We are in the Rousseauist tradition that maintains a belief in the essential goodness of man. We feel that man has certain drives or instincts that are basically good, i.e., natural to man, and that education should capitalize upon these instincts, such as the instinct for curiosity, and help them to grow. We feel that there are many damaging outside influences and that many children are prevented from exercising a natural tendency toward education because of such influences. Because we feel that man is good, we think that we can give him a great deal of freedom. In progressivism there is no authoritarian teacher, no harsh code of discipline to be administered, and certainly no corporal punishment. We feel that even things like religion or books can be used as ways of punishing children, or at least making them unhappy, and we have no feeling that books, facts, religion, or anything else has to be made a part of the educational program. We think that when a child's instincts are not thwarted or corrupted he will be a wise chooser of what is best for him. We do believe in the use of the teacher for guidance just as Emile[3] had his tutor, but primarily we feel that the child teaches himself. The teacher as a guide merely tries to arrange the learning situation so that the child maximizes his opportunity for learning. We do this without coercion, without punishment, without the need to do things because they may be good later on. Indeed, we feel that the child will do them because he sees their use right now, and if he doesn't, then perhaps they shouldn't be done at all, or else done later."

"But my knowledge of progressivism," said Estabrook, "leads me to see it as a very disciplined education. I mean under the best conditions the children are all busily working."

"That's true," answered the progressivist.

---

[2] The *Lord of the Flies* by William Golding (G. P. Putnam & Sons, 1954) deals with English school boys who are abandoned on a deserted island and who become, without the constraints of civilization, increasingly savage and cannibalistic.

[3] *Emile* was written by Jean-Jacques Rousseau (New York: E. P. Dutton and Co., 1930). Originally published in 1762, *Emile* deals with the special tutoring required for a "natural" education.

"Then, I mean, you do place some validity upon work, upon being busy."

"Yes, but these things are natural and desirable to man," answered Price. "They are not the result of us putting work and business into man. Unfortunately, most education bores people so much they lose interest. They want fun, and when they see that education can be fun they get very involved in it."

"I guess you are tired of hearing the charge that you progressivists are clever manipulators," said Pennington, "but I think you are. I must admit your effectiveness. We think that people have a need for work too, but we sometimes feel that you motivate them to work on things beneath what they can really do."

"Yes, I agree with that," said Estabrook. "That's what we mean by all these fads and frills. You have them working and busily engaged in nonsensical tasks."

"I don't see how you can say they are nonsensical," said Price, "if the person doing them thinks they are valuable. If a person is interested in something, then shouldn't he be encouraged in it?"

"Then suppose he is interested in pornography," asked Pennington, "does that mean that you would encourage his interest in that subject?"

"I would try to utilize his interest in pornography to interest him in other things, such as aesthetics," replied Price. "This is where the importance of the teacher comes in."

"Then you do admit to manipulating students?" said Estabrook.

"I don't like the word manipulate," replied Price. "We do feel that a person's instincts should find some outlet, and if a child expresses certain interests then we help him fulfill them. We are not necessarily opposed to pornography or anything else."

"I think your last statement shows why we have been reacting so strongly against your philosophy," stated Estabrook. "You have undermined the traditional subjects by letting children study things they are interested in, and you know that their interests are rather low-level unless directed higher."

"I know nothing of the sort," said Price. "I think that ordinarily a child would not be interested in pornography unless he were somehow warped by having neurotic parents or a neurotic teacher. Basically, we think that a child's interests are very normal ones that need to be encouraged, not thwarted."

"I want to say that I am mostly in agreement with the progressivist on his feelings about man's basic nature," said Reed. "We feel that man is basically good, that he can be trusted, that his aspirations should find some outlet in society as a whole. It is not man we feel is the culprit, but society, his environment. Because the environment is corrupting, man becomes corrupted. What we are promoting is a change in the environment to bring it more in line with what man's basic nature really is. We think, for example, that most present forms of government tend to corrupt and distort man's basic good sense of values, and that if an environment is set up that is more natural to man then he will tend to act more intelligently and honestly."

"But who created the present environment if it was not man?" asked Extan.

"Yes, but man created it out of a good heart, and it turned against him," replied the reconstructionist. "I'm sure that you realize the strong effect of environment. Man created things he thought would be of help to him, but they turned out to be harmful. Consequently, we need to reassess the entire system and bring it more in line with the real desires of mankind, a desire for peace, for example, as well as justice and order."

"You said that you agreed basically with the progressivist, and then you go on to stress something that sounds entirely different," said Estabrook.

"I said that we both believe man is basically good," answered Reed. "The issue of difference is whether man is going to continue to proceed in a piecemeal way to correct the situation that thwarts his natural goodness, or whether he is going to grapple with it in terms of the whole society. We feel that a major overhaul of society is necessary, whereas we think that the progressivist promotes answers that are only intermediate to the problem. Although we are basically utopian, we are not romantic utopians. We know the cold hard world. But we want to change it into something better, something that will allow man to release his natural impulses for good."

"The thing is," said Price, "that utopian proposals have never worked. They always fall down some way. Although you might think that you see your ends as intermediate and flexible, they tend to become absolutes, and therein lies the seeds of your destruction, for you cannot change things to fit new events and ideas. Our idea of progress is open-ended so that we can adjust to new developments, whether technological or social."

"But if you don't have some sense of direction," answered Reed, "you won't know when you get there. We feel that ends can be kept open-ended too, but we feel that you need some kind of direction, even if only tentative. Getting back to the point, however, we do think that man is basically good, that he can be trusted, that one can proceed democratically, and that there should be an end to repression in both society and education. Although we know that some so-called utopian societies have been repressive, we don't think that they need to be. I really think that we have more faith in man than anyone here because we are not afraid of what he may do in the future. If anything, we want to rush the future, and we think that it will be better than what we have now."

"That smacks of Hegelianism,"[4] said Estabrook. "The future can be worse, and will be if we don't harness our present resources in useful ways. I think we need to think more about what goes on now. We have enough problems at present without thinking about the problems of the future."

"I believe we do have to consider the future," said Beattie, "but in more practical terms than the reconstructionist. He has some vague notion about the future as a state of mind, as a way of orienting people toward change. The kind of future I see is based upon practical applications of current technology. But to answer your question about man, and I think it is a very important question, we feel that man is really neither good or bad, but rather neutral. We feel that we can make man good or bad simply by controlling his experiences, which Locke intimates in his notion of the mind as a *tabula rasa*.[5] Well, we subscribe to that in great part, that is, that most of what man is is a product of his experiences. What passes for conscience, for example, are simply the kinds of experiences you have had about good and evil, experiences you may have gotten from books, actual personal experiences, or reflection. Your attitude toward certain foods, dress, and love-making, are all a product of experience. So that if one controls a person's experiences he therefore controls the person. Experience also includes reflection and though we cannot control reflection completely, we can control what sensations you might reflect about, and in that sense control reflection too. For example, let us assume that I take a young child up to an isolated section of the Far North and I teach him that everything you think is good is bad, and everything you think bad is good. I teach him that stealing, lying, and hurting people is good, and I reward him when he does these things. That way he will continue to do them. I cannot see why he would think these things were not good unless he were to encounter other experiences, peers, books, or what have you, that would decon-

[4]Georg Wilhelm Hegel (1770–1831) was a German philosopher who believed that all ideas and institutions were evolving manifestations of God trying to understand himself.

[5]John Locke (1632–1704) believed that the mind at birth was a blank tablet, a "tabula rasa", and that all ideas came from sensation and reflection.

dition him. But to think that there might be something innate that would interfere with such conditioning is ridiculous. There is nothing there."

"Nothing but the mind itself," said Pennington. "What about that? I mean what causes the mind to order and synthesize things? What categorizes what one knows?"

"Yes, I read Kant[6] too," said Beattie. "But what Kant did not recognize is that the ability to order, the ability to create, and all the rest, is also learned, and it is learned from experience. It is not a priori. The brain is really like a computer. What you call mind are ideas that are put into the computer. You program the mind, so to speak, with experiences. Thus, if you put order in, you will get order out. If you program disorder, you will get disorder. It is as simple as that. Whatever you program into the computer is all you can get out. There is nothing extra there at all."

"What about instincts?" asked Price. "Aren't there certain instincts that an individual has that are not programmed?"

"Absolutely not," said Beattie. "Instincts are also learned. They are a lower-level learning to be sure, but they are a part of the learning that man has accomplished on his path from a mere animal to man. Take for example the kind of reflex which small children have, and which enables them to grasp objects very strongly. This was probably learned when man was still an ape as a way of clinging to the mother so that he would not be blown out of the tree. We have to consider all of our past experiences, no matter how far back they go, as learning experiences."

"You said a while back that the mind was like a computer," said Reed. "But even a computer has wires and wheels and tubes that exist prior to the information that is programmed in."

"That's true, but I would not call these ideas," responded Beattie. "Man also has an elaborate computer with cells and cortex and all the rest, but so far as any ideas go there are none there until programming begins, so that to the same extent you are working with a blank tablet or an empty machine."

"If I may pick up at this point," interrupted Extan, "I am quite bewildered by the simplicity of it all. It so explains away everything: Hate, absurdity, religion, and all the rest can be blamed upon environment, or as you say, experience. We do not deny that man can be conditioned and that we are all conditioned to some extent. But we

---

[6]Immanuel Kant (1724–1804) questioned Locke's view of the mind as a passive instrument. Kant believed that the mind was a dynamic force in shaping, classifying, and ordering our ideas.

feel that man is often responsible for his own conditioning by allowing himself to be conditioned. I am saying that 'other-directed' people do allow themselves to be conditioned, but we would hope that education, if conducted in a free manner, would enable man to resist such conditioning, to understand it, and hence to rise above it. All of us know how easy it would be to give in to the conditioning of the establishment. But we also think that man can resist such influences and become an authentic and 'inner-directed' person. We think this is true even when man is rewarded for becoming 'other-directed.' Man is not a computer, he is a man. To think about man as a computer is to begin to destroy what he is. We see man as a creature of emotions, instincts, paradoxes, and other things. We see him very much the animal, often acting irrationally, often acting in ways that harm himself and others. But we also feel that he can be rational, committed, and courageous, and that these things are not easily put into a test-tube and analyzed. Basically, we feel that man is free, or relatively free, and that man should strive to become freer and more productive. Thus, we get down to what man is. We don't like pat answers like good, bad, or neutral. To some extent he is all of these. Man is not something that you can label and then say he is that. He is too complex a creature. Certainly, man may be neutral in some way, but in other ways he is not. There is still much of the animal in man which needs to be taken into account, and there is still much about man that cannot be described adequately at all."

"You complain about my being too simplistic in explaining man," replied the behavioral engineer, "but I never found any real value in things being complex either. You explain man as being this highly complex paradoxical creature. But what we find complex or paradoxical, or 'absurd,' as you often refer to it, is what he has been programmed with, whether it be by society, his parents, peers, or what have you. Indeed, your philosophy programs man to some extent, as do all philosophies."

"What we object to is your desire to explain man away," said Extan. "Yours is really a circular argument. You explain everything as a part of conditioning, so that if one goes against certain kinds of conditioning it is because he has been conditioned against it. We think it might be because man is human and can assert his man-like qualities to place himself in situations that were not conditioned in him, but were done because of his own free choice."

"There is no such thing as freedom," said Beattie. "Ideas about freedom are all programmed. If a person is taught consistently that such and such is freedom he will no doubt believe it."

"There may not be any such thing as perfect freedom, I warrant you," said Extan. "But some acts are more free than others, and a man can perform free acts if he chooses. His very act of choosing to do so is what makes him a man, an individual. Let us take homosexuality, for example. I think all homosexuals have been programmed with the idea that homosexuality is bad, and yet we find many of them now speaking out and saying they're homosexuals and that's that. It's an act of freedom whether one agrees with the attitude or not."

"They're receiving a reward from somewhere," said Beattie, "from each other perhaps."

"I don't think that everything can be explained in terms of rewards either," said Extan, "and if they could then society should be changed so that men do not act only for rewards but because of the way they think they should act. We need to make our schools places where people can exercise free choice, not where they are conditioned to act so and so."

"We can condition them to act freely," said Beattie, "or at least to believe they are acting freely."

"No," said Extan. "It's not the same thing at all. We don't want man conditioned. We want him to waver between choices. We want him to have conflict, anxiety. We don't want a push-button thinker. Too much education is that way already. There are a lot of things we don't like, particularly this idea of turning man into a robot."

"I wish you would follow that up," said Price. "You said that there were a lot of things you didn't like. Maybe if you would start we could all point out various things we don't like either."

"Yes, I'd be glad to," said the existentialist. "To begin with, we don't like who controls the schools. They are in the hands of the 'Others,'[7] not in the hands of those who go there. There are numerous studies to show that the real decision-making in education is made at the top, not by the rank and file. We feel that the students should run the schools, and that the community should take a part in this too. We object to having schools run by school boards and boards of trustees, which ultimately means by the corporation, since so many who direct our educational institutions are also managers of large corporations. There are studies showing that those who do serve on school boards and act as trustees are the most conservative members of society, if not ultra-conservative. Needless to say, this

---

[7]For further discussion of the "Others" or "other-directedness" as related to education see *Introduction to the Philosophy of Education* by George F. Kneller (New York: John Wiley, 1964) pp. 61–64.

explains why the schools so much reflect the status quo and the most traditional kinds of values. It explains why patriotism is so fostered, religion, business interests, and all the rest. We also feel that the school is run for the interest and profit of the establishment. If you look in your school newspapers, even on the elementary level, you will see ads for products of all kinds. If the students can't afford them at this time, at least they're being made ready to buy them at a future time. Also, the school is used for the purpose of turning out the required number of doctors, lawyers, engineers, and teachers we need to keep the system going."

"You make it sound like a great plot," said Estabrook.

"It is not a conscious or well-planned plot, but it amounts to the same thing. People have a lot of selfish inhumane motives and they use the schools as ways to satisfy them. The school becomes a part of the conspiracy, as it were—the military-industrial-academic complex. People are encouraged to go to school so that they can become a part of the establishment, not only to make money, but to buy products, and to lead an affluent middle-class life. This warps people's values. Another fault of the school is that it promotes all of this belongingness, togetherness, and groupness, we hear so much about. Like the lemmings everyone has to go along, be a part of what's happening, no matter how inane it is. Whether the progressivists are responsible for this or not—and we think they are to some extent— it is still true that the schools, in overemphasizing group activity, have often overlooked the individual. We feel that individuals need to be fostered by the schools, that we need creative intelligent people, but that instead, people are molded to fit some mean. We are not opposed to groups if individuals join groups because of their personal commitment, but too often we find they are sucked into them simply because they have been made to feel too insecure without the group. Unfortunately, there are many educators who think that the purpose of the school is to do away with insecurity, with tension, with anxiety. Very seldom is death mentioned, or perversion; even sex was not discussed until recently because it was felt that such topics would bother children and they might not sleep at night. In other words we've been hiding life from them. The tragic is a side of life too, and we feel that children should be given some sense of tragedy beginning at a very early age."

"How would you do this?" asked Reed.

"To begin with, we see no sense in hitting the children over the head with tragedy before they are ready for it, but if a child's grandfather or someone else he knows should die, we can't see covering it up by saying that he passed away, or that he has gone on a long trip, or any of those other things we say to children. We think you should say that he died, that his heart stopped beating or whatever happened, and if the child wants to know more, or is curious, then go on and talk about what happens after death in terms of decomposition and so on."

"How about an afterlife?" asked Pennington. "Would you discuss that too?"

"We might," said Extan. "We would not be averse to saying that some people believe in an afterlife and that they believe certain things will happen. I think it might even be appropriate to take children to see the city morgue. That way they could come to their own views as to what death is like. You see, in education we are always covering up. We do not want to show people reality because reality is brutish, cruel, hard. We take children down to see the police station, and when we do, it has been cleaned up the night before. All the drunks have been removed from the tank, no one is being beaten by the rubber hose. But I think that if we want to really give children an idea of what the police are like we should go there during the height of their police activities when drunks are being booked, and when there are obscenities, blood and violence."

"I think you might be able to explain those things without having them see them," said Estabrook.

"You might," replied the existentialist. "But I think my method would be much more appropriate and realistic. Often people disguise things with words. There is a tendency to romanticize poverty, death, and war. It is not romantic for those experiencing it, but it is often couched in language that makes it sound not so bad. The kind of education we would like to see is one which develops an awareness of slums, poverty, hate, disease, the evils of warfare, and all the other things not generally discussed in education."

"You make it sound like education should wallow in the mud," said Pennington.

"It should wallow in the mud of life, as much as it revels in the perfume of life," answered Extan. "There is mud and people should know about it. Another thing that we are very concerned about," said the existentialist, "is the emphasis that education still places on reason. From Plato on up through the 1900s there was great emphasis placed on man's ability to use reason to solve all problems. It is not surprising that pragmatism has so much captured the American imagination as a philosophy since it is generally thought of as an open-ended, optimistic and reasonable philosophy. But ever since

World War II there has been a steady penetrating analysis of reason, and I think that we are beginning to find that reason is not that great golden instrument we thought it was, and that instead of solving problems it often creates greater ones. What really controls men's actions, we feel, is not so much reason as instinct and emotion. We think that man uses reason as a way of rationalizing what his instincts or emotions direct him to do. Look at war, for example. Man has continually gone from war to war and given good reasons for each. The history books are always replete with explanations in terms of ideology, religion, and economics. But the real reason may be that man simply is a hostile aggressive creature who likes to fight and if we don't come to grips with that realization we will continue to go from war to war."

"You debunk reason," said Estabrook. "Yet it was reason that told you that reason was suspect."

"Yes, I realize that," answered Extan. "And indeed I could be wrong. But I think that we can use reason to study reason just as we might use one computer to study another computer, or a computer to study itself, or to redesign itself, in fact. We are not opposed to reason so long as man understands that there are other factors shaping his development, such as emotions, which often direct his behavior more than reason."

"How would you translate this into educational terms?" asked Beattie. "I mean the idea that man may be directed more by emotion than reason."

"We feel that educators should stop looking at man as a machine, and begin to look at him as a feeling as well as a thinking creature," replied Extan. "We believe that it is just because education and business look upon man so much as a machine that he tends to act like a machine. It is a self-fulfilling prophecy. We think that if education tended to look and respond to man as man, as a free individual, that this would help to lead him in that direction. We also think that educators need to deal more with man as an emotional creature, i.e., as a being who hates and loves, and often indulges in aggression, and that people should be made aware of this fact instead of trying to hide it. We feel that with awareness, man would also be encouraged to utilize these emotions in ways that are constructive and humane rather than as they are at present, destructive and inhumane. We might have dances, for example, athletic contests, even competitiveness, and we would encourage people to find ways of utilizing these kinds of emotions in useful ways."

"We progressivists have always dealt with man as an instinctive being," said Price. "Dewey pointed out that the child had such instincts as curiosity which the school could foster and promote. He was well aware too that the school often dulls such natural instincts."

"I am aware of that," said Extan. "But I feel that you still place too much emphasis on the child learning to problem-solve, which might make him successful in contemporary terms, but his insistence on solving a problem may make him solve it at great social and emotional cost. We would like to think that children would be given some feeling that not all problems can be solved, such as the problem of death, perhaps even the problem of war."

"I certainly would like to take issue with you here," said Beattie.

"So would I," said Reed.

"You said," responded the behavioral engineer, "that children should be given a sense of tragedy. I could agree to this. I might even add that they should be given some awareness of luck in life, and perhaps you remember the story of the soups in *Walden Two* where those who win the toss of a coin sit down to eat their soup first. I fear that your insistence on tragedy could well be overdone, however. We think that there is a tragic side to life and a happy side, but some of us feel that we have had considerable success in reducing the tragic and improving the other. The conquest of disease is an example, or take the gradual elimination of poverty, etc. We are moving in ways that will provide a better life for everyone, and you sound like some Cassandra who is preaching doom. There need not be doom, you know."

"I quite agree with the behavioral engineer," said Reed. "The value of utopia is that it is a state of mind that makes you see how much better things can be. I don't think we can eliminate every single sense of discord and ugliness, but we can do a better job than we are doing now. We can create a better world, and man needs to be infused with the idea that he can. A sense of tragedy could be a very limiting factor in moving ahead resolutely. It would be something always saying no, or something that stresses a pessimistic rather than an optimistic attitude toward life."

"The trouble with most utopias is that they do not make room for trouble or discontent or tragedy," said Extan. "They are too pat, too machine-like, too perfect. Life isn't like that, nor need it be. We are not looking forward to the programmed world with programmed tragedy, and the three minutes of hate found in *1984*.[8] But we do

---

[8] *1984* by George Orwell (New York: Harcourt, Brace and Co., 1949) is a dysutopia which presents a frightening picture of totalitarian control in the future.

want a world of realism. Man need not wallow in tragedy, but what evil or unhappiness exists should be acknowledged and dealt with. The bad side of life deserves the same amount of attention we give the good."

"I fear," said Pennington, "that when you say realism, you don't mean realism at all, because realism also means gardens, parks, and smiling people, and you are always asking us to go over and look at the slums and visit leper hospitals and see people killing each other. Such things happen, but so do good things."

"We don't deny that there are a lot of good things, but we feel that these are already stressed enough," said Extan. "When visitors come to town I know I can count on you taking them to see the beautiful museums, parks, and houses. I am not sure I can count on you taking them to see the slums, the filth, the inhumanity that exists. Likewise in education, I know that teachers will expose their wards to the good and the beautiful, but will they do the same for the bad and the ugly? If we seem to overemphasize the latter it is only because we feel that the former is being taken care of by a large number of other people. Look at the readers that children use, for example. Look at your Dick and Jane living in suburbia where they don't fight or go to the bathroom; they have outstandingly good looking parents without any money problems, never get sick, and so on. Compare this with *Peanuts,* for example, which I think exhibits a much more existential approach. Charlie Brown often feels inferior, Lucy has a castration complex, Linus needs his security blanket, Snoopy has delusions of grandeur. It is much more realistic, though some of you might say childhood isn't like that. I think it is."

"I think that the existentialist has presented us with strong and lucid arguments," said Beattie, "but I think his views are based more on his ability to persuade than upon the facts. I would therefore like to respond to his arguments, and in so doing, point out some of the objections we have of contemporary education. The existentialist says that we need anxiety in education, a sense of tragedy, more emphasis on feeling, and so on. These are all reasonable, I suppose, in light of what man is. But I do not find them reasonable in the light of what man can be. The existentialist takes it for granted, for example, that man will always be aggressive, inhumane, perhaps even perverted. We feel that such things, whether instinctive or not, can be changed. The existentialist seems to feel that man can change his ideas but not his instincts. We find this to be untrue. We can change man's instincts too, and we do it all the time with animals. We feel that the reason why people are aggressive or inhumane is not so much due to something they were born with as it was with something they learned. They might have learned it during toilet training when as children they were forced to do something they didn't want to do, or it might have been during any number of other situations. Since one learned it, he can also unlearn it, and we feel that given the right environment with the right kinds of rewards for the right kinds of things, we can, for all intents and purposes, eliminate those things that the existentialist seems to feel are uneliminable. We realize that there have been attempts in government, in religion, and other institutions to change man, and that these have failed only because there was no awareness of the methods of control. As our existentialist pointed out, this has mostly been an attempt to control individuals through an appeal to reason. This was not effective. Our control is not over reason, however, but over the basic kinds of responses common to all animals. We can control man's behavior in ways that will eliminate inhumanity, and this is not something in the far future, but something we can do now if people want to utilize this force."

"It sounds like *Brave New World*,"[9] said Pennington.

"It may be a kind of *Brave New World*, but one without the negative characteristics. What is wrong with control, with planning, with the elimination of evils?"

"Isn't that what Hitler tried to do?" asked Estabrook. "At least as he saw it?"

"In a way Hitler was a conditionist. He recognized that man has all of those murky things inside of him that Extan recognizes, and he used them through midnight torch parades, music, and other things that directed the emotions in ways that he wanted. But although such forces can be harnessed for evil, we can also harness them for good, and can create utopia in our time. We recognize the evolutionary factors that have gone into making man what he is. We know what he has come through in terms of superstition, violence, survival, and other things. But instead of giving in to these things, or even instead of trying to understand them, which we find very difficult to do, we can change people without knowing why they are the way they are. Take an example from psychoanalysis. The traditional method of psychoanalysis was to try to find out why the patient acted in such and such a way. This brought you into contact with Oedipal theories, penis envy, castration complexes, and all the rest, and maybe you

---

[9] *Brave New World* by Aldous Huxley (London, England: Chatto and Windus, 1932). This is another dysutopia picturing extreme control over an individual's hereditary and environmental influences.

found the answer and maybe you didn't. And even when you found the cause for the patient's behavior he still might not change it. But now, we find we don't need to know the cause. We can change the patient's behavior without knowing why he acted the way he did. It's the same way in terms of society. We don't have to know why society got this way in order to change it."

"What does this mean in terms of what the schools do?" asked Price.

"We agree with the existentialist that reason has been oversold," replied Beattie. "We are constantly trying to reason people into accepting this or that, and sometimes we can and sometimes we can't. We don't need to appeal to man's reason to get him to act this way or that way. We feel that the schools are monumentally ineffective in knowing how to control behavior just because they *do* try to persuade people to do things through reason. We think that every teacher should be familiar with the essentials of behavioral engineering and know how to apply it in terms of effective classroom practice. We think that we need to decide at the highest levels of society what kind of people we want and then utilize our educational methods toward achieving that end. We don't seem to know at the present time what goals we should be working for, either in education or in society as a whole, and this engenders a kind of laissez-faire attitude toward education that we feel is somewhat disheartening. Not to use conditioning in education is somewhat akin to a Christian Scientist's refusing a splint for a broken leg. We think we are making some progress, however, and we do see the time coming, a little more every day, when conditioning will become a reality on a large scale. I must say that I see it as the only answer to ending the kind of dreadful things everyone here has mentioned. What upsets us greatly, too, is the amount of conditioning that is going on and has always been going on to condition people in negative ways. In countless schools throughout this country children are daily being conditioned to conform, to be belligerent, competitive, and successful. They are being conditioned by their schools, parents, church, and society as a whole. We decry the fact that this great power is being so misused. We see it as a tool for good, but mostly, it has been used as a tool for evil. Look at how people are conditioned by advertisements that equate cigarettes with springtime, cars with sex, and entice you to buy products that are not only not good for you, but are downright harmful. We think that during this interim phase while we're waiting for society to decide where it should go that the schools could at least neutralize this kind of conditioning."

"I would like to interrupt to say that I don't see what is so wrong with society or the school taking a laissez-faire attitude as you call it," said Estabrook. "I like diversity, even with methods. Why do we all have to decide on only one way to do something."

"We don't believe that diversity has to be eliminated, nor do we have to agree as a body on all things," replied Beattie. "We only have to agree on a few things that I think most men are in agreement with already—at least in theory—that is, an end to war, hunger, and illiteracy. Why don't we make such agreements as starting points for a new and better society?"

"People are wary of being made to do something—even if it's for their own good," said Price, "and I'm not sure they should anyway."

"Hopefully, we will reach a point," said the behavioral engineer, "where people will themselves readily consent to certain kinds of conditioning for ends that they see are necessary. For example, one might consciously condition himself not to smoke, or to do a certain amount of useful work. He realizes that he is conditioning himself, but he is doing it for a certain desired end. I think, or at least, I hope, that man will realize that he has to condition himself not to fight, not to steal from others, or not to go through a red light. That it is for his own good, as well as for the good of others."

"I have no objection to a person conditioning himself," said Extan. "It's when other people do it for him that I object."

"I sympathize with that view," said Beattie. "But I still think it's a question of whether you really do want to improve people or not. If you do, then this is the only way I see that we can do it. The existentialist and I are at least in agreement that you can't appeal to people's reason as a way of doing it."

"Gentlemen," interrupted Pennington, who was looking at his watch, "I believe we agreed to stop for dinner at this hour. Let's return to this point at our next session."

Questions for Discussion

1. Is there any value in moving into new issues until answers are found for the problems that have been raised already?

2. Comment on Estabrook's statement that some students will select a tough academic program but many others will take the easy way out if you let them. (p. 29)

3. Do you agree with Pennington that we need to integrate things like philosophy and poetry on every level of schooling? (p. 33)

4. Do you agree with Pennington that "programmed philosophers" is a contradiction in terms? (p. 36)

5. Do you agree with Estabrook (p. 37) that most people are not ready for the ideas of the behavioral engineer? Explain.

6. What is your reaction to Reed's proposal for future schooling? (pp. 38–40)

7. Do you agree with Beattie (p. 41) that perhaps most of the classics present the view that man is evil? Support or attack this view.

8. How would you evaluate Reed's argument that man created his environment out of a good heart but that it turned against him? (p. 45) Is this reminiscent of any other position you know?

3

The Third Day

"One of the things that seems to bother a lot of people," said Extan, "is that philosophers—educational philosophers as well as other kinds of philosophers—never seem to come to any agreement about what they believe. I think that although there are points here and there where *we* seem to converge, overall I would say that there are more basic disagreements between us than agreements."

"That's to be expected, isn't it?" replied Price. "When Edwards got us all together for this conference he deliberately chose competing educational philosophies. I would have been quite surprised if we didn't have a spirited debate."

"I often hear the statement that philosophers never agree," added Pennington, "but it is one of those clichés applied to philosophy by people who don't know anything about it. How would great systems like Christianity and Communism, Stoicism, Epicureanism, and Pragmatism have arisen if there had not been fundamental agreement upon some basic points? I would certainly point out that to create enduring philosophical systems that last hundreds of years certainly implies agreement somewhere."

"Yes, that is certainly true and needs to be pointed out," said Estabrook. "There has been a great deal of agreement among philosophers, but who wants to hear the same thing over and over? We tend to choose someone who best represents that system and then let him be the spokesman for it. This is not without its difficulties, and I'm not even trying to defend it, I am just pointing out that historically it has been true."

"As you say, letting one philosopher speak for all in the system, is not without its problems," said Extan. "Existentialists are very sensitive about being categorized, grouped, and labeled, but it is done to us all the time. Existentialists are lumped together, whether they be atheistic or theistic existentialists."

"Although there is a great deal of disagreement in philosophical thinking," said Reed, "I think this is to be expected, and is as it should be. As the essentialist points out, you don't want to hear the same thing over and over. Philosophy presents us with alternative beliefs. It is the different view that we are interested in: the new way of looking at things."

"I think," said Beattie, "that you should specify that this is how philosophers feel. I don't believe that the average man on the street is interested in alternative viewpoints, and he does tend to see a great deal of confusion in philosophical thinking."

"Yes, I agree with that," said the reconstructionist. "I don't even believe it is true of all philosophers, but I think that generally speaking we, as philosophers, are interested in ideas and that we are very critical of the ideas we have. We like to have our ideas explored, and even exploded."

"Yes, sometimes," said Pennington, "as long as it isn't too often." (Laughter.)

"Perhaps it might be fruitful," said Price, "if we were to point out just how we see the relationship of philosophy to education. I am not sure at this point whether some of you see educational philosophy as an outgrowth of other philosophical systems or whether you see it as a unique philosophy in itself."

"I think this might be quite useful at this point," said Estabrook, "since we have willy-nilly gotten into this area."

"Let me try then," said Pennington, "to clarify what we, or perhaps I should say, what I think at this point, since there are varying views on perennialism just as there are various interpretations of existentialism. But, to begin with, we do subscribe to a literal translation of the Greek word 'philosophy' in that it is 'the love of wisdom.' We think that philosophies that are engaged in telling you

how to build something, whether it be new machines or new societies, are not philosophies per se."

"I hate to interrupt here," said Reed, "but didn't Plato, whom I
know you admire, propose the building of a new society in the
Republic?"

"Yes, but I'm talking about construction in terms of architecture,
wood panels, shrubbery and things like that. Plato created the idea
for a new society which is quite a different thing from creating it in
terms of its material form."

"Right away we run into the problem that Aristotle faced," said the
essentialist, "and that is that it is difficult, if not impossible, to separate the idea from the material thing, but I'll let it pass until
later."

"Thank you," replied Pennington. "We do feel that Plato exemplified the kind of approach to philosophy known to you as Idealism
and which is exemplified in a perennialist philosophy of education.
What that means, principally, is that we feel that ideas are more
important than material things."

"Didn't Plato believe that material things didn't exist anyway,"
asked Price, "that it was all illusion?"

"Yes, that's true," said Pennington. "Material things were, for
Plato, simply copies of ideas. Since they are copies and not the real
thing, Plato questioned why one should study copies and not the idea
or forms they came from. I cannot help recalling at this point Plato's
'Allegory of the Cave' where, as you know, the prisoner frees himself
from the world of illusion or materiality and proceeds upward on the
ascent to truth or spirituality. However, if I can gauge the intent of
your question I would say that although perennialists take varying
views on the reality of matter, they all are in agreement that ideas
are more important than matter. The ideas in a book, for example,
are more important than its cover, or paper, or print."

"Not some of the best-sellers I've been reading," said Estabrook.

"Well, they should be," said Pennington. "This is why we put such
an emphasis on the Great Books. It isn't because of their binding, or
even because they are old, but rather, because they contain great
ideas. When we translate this into educational terms we are not
opposed to teachers taking their students on field trips or studying
material things under a microscope or anything else, but we do feel
that whatever studies there are, they should lead to something higher
than the material components themselves. Education should lead us
toward great ideas, and not only to the great ideas of the past, but
to the creation of more great ideas."

"Would you say that the program at St. John's in Annapolis[1] represents the kind of education program you perennialists would like to have?" asked Beattie.

"Yes, I would say so," answered Pennington. "As you know, at St. John's the curriculum revolves around the classics. If you want to know about philosophy you study Plato, Aristotle, Kant, Nietzsche, etc. If you want to know about psychology you study Pavlov and Freud. If you want to know about science you study Newton, Darwin, and Galileo."

"All those that you mentioned died quite some time ago," said Price.

"Yes, that's true. But their ideas are still important for us to know. They are still valuable. We are too much caught up, I think, by catchwords like 'relevance.' Some of the ideas that were created a long time ago are much more relevant to today's problems than ideas that were created yesterday. Take, for example, the problem of the individual versus the state, i.e., what rights does the individual have, and what rights does the state have? This problem, which we are wrestling with today, was a problem that many thinkers in the past dealt with extensively, such as Plato and Jesus, and I would say that their answers are not only better but more relevant to the problem than any other answers that I have heard. But to answer you more directly, at St. John's they do deal with modern writers like Hemingway and Faulkner, as well as modern scientists like Skinner and Bohr. It is only that we are selective about what we consider really worthwhile. We don't think that just because someone can put something down on paper and get it published it is worthwhile. In fact we find great difficulty in wading through the trash being published today to get to the few good ideas that are there."

"I think that our perennialist has presented a quite impassioned argument," said Estabrook, "and I even found it somewhat persuasive myself. After all, who is in favor of trash?" (Laughter.) "But, I do have some serious objections not only as to the roots of his philosophy, but also as to how that philosophy should be applied educationally. As I mentioned earlier, part of my argument stems from the Platonic-Aristotelian controversy where Aristotle believed matter to be real, and was therefore a Realist rather than an Idealist. Rather than being illusory as Plato suggests, Aristotle believed that matter was actually capable of teaching us a great deal about the world in

---

[1]St. John's College, Annapolis, Maryland, offers a program of study with no majors, teaching by "recitation tutorials and discussion seminars" which revolve around a study of the Great Books.

which we live and, further, that it could stimulate us toward the creation or discovery of new ideas. We feel, therefore, that an understanding of what the world is and how it works is the first step in understanding who we are, and what we should do. I should like to point out here also, that many of those who were Aristotelians, such as St. Thomas, put great stress on a study of matter as something you could use to advance to spirituality. If you look at St. Thomas' five proofs of God's existence, for example, they all depend on sense observation. But, and I think I am speaking here for most essentialists, we do not believe that a study of matter is necessarily transcendental as St. Thomas suggests. We do agree that matter helps to produce ideas, but we do not suggest that ideas carry with them any spiritual connotation, and may be in fact, and probably are, material things themselves. What I am saying is that we emphasize the side of Aristotle that is concerned with a scientific view of the world rather than that side which seems to lead to religion. We do think that a study of matter encourages philosophical reflection, however, and if you look at most scientific bulletins today, such as *The Bulletin of Atomic Physicists*, you will see that scientists are becoming increasingly concerned with the philosophical questions that their investigations engender, such as 'Why are we here?' and 'Who made us?', which are equally important questions for a scientist or a philosopher. It is true that Aristotle was a deductionist, and that he also made many disastrous scientific statements, but we trace his concern for empirical studies through the modern scientific movement with Bacon, Locke, and others. We essentialists are basically empirical people. We have nothing against theory, and indeed we think that theory is the beginning of knowledge. But, in terms of what is true, we want to see proofs. We want some kind of justification for what we believe, and until theories are proven they remain just what they are, theories."

"I would like to point out," said Pennington, "that you mentioned Bacon and Locke as beginning the modern movement in science, or at least giving it some kind of philosophical justification, but do you remember where such thinking led? It culminated in the Idealism of Berkeley and in the skepticism of Kant and Hume. In effect, what they were saying, is that although you have some kind of animal faith that matter exists, it would be very hard to prove it in any absolute sense, and that whatever proof you use is trying to prove matter with matter. I should like to raise one more point also. We perennialists do not agree that ideas are material. We think they are non-material, and in the thinking of some perennialists, they are spiritual. Since so-called empirical investigations can only be known in terms of ideas, and we can only know things through ideas, we cannot be certain that anything exists other than ideas. This is basically the Platonic-Aristotelian argument you mentioned, and as I have already indicated, I side with Plato in this respect."

"I will grant you," said Estabrook, "that in terms of proving anything ultimately, we cannot be sure of our beliefs. This is perhaps why many essentialists are skeptical about absolutes like God and heaven, though this is not true of all essentialists. We take a rather 'common sense' attitude about the world. If you wish to use Santayana's term and call it 'animal faith' that is all right with me, but I would say that basically, we accept what our senses tell us to be true. We realize that the way one man sees red may not be the same way another sees it, but if they come to some common understanding about the color of things, then for all practical purposes they each know what red is. We think that many philosophers create problems that do not exist, that instead of accepting sense data they point out that one cannot be sure that it exists or that it exists as we see it. We know that. But we find that those same philosophers still act as though it existed, and they certainly use matter in terms of eating and breathing. We are aware that science is built upon certain unprovable axioms, but we think you have to start somewhere, and we start with the reality of matter and the use of sense perceptions."

"I think it would help," said Reed, "if you would translate what all this means in terms of educational consequences. We have some idea of what Realists believe, but how does this relate to essentialism, and to either a philosophical or an anti-philosophical view?"

"It is not an anti-philosophical view at all," replied Estabrook. "I have been trying to point out that our view of the world, and education, rests on as strong a philosophical base as any of the rest of you. It is too much in the current thinking of people, particularly philosophers, to think that if you favor science and promote science that you are therefore opposed to philosophy. We believe, as did Aristotle, that there is a complementarity between philosophy and science in which one overlaps with the other. Darwin's discoveries, for example, not only assisted in giving us greater scientific knowledge, but helped to answer some of our philosophical questions about the world as well. All scientific discoveries have philosophical import, and I would even contend that science has assisted us more in providing answers to so-called philosophical questions than have philosophy and religion. Look at how Galileo punctured the theory held by philosophers and theologians that the earth was the center of the universe. Look at how anthropologists and geologists have caused a reassessment of ideas about Adam and Eve, or the conception of the world as only some 4,000 years old. I listened intently to what the perennialist said about reading the Great Books, even about great scientific books, but we don't take the view that science is something that only happened in the past. We think that some answers can be found in the Great Books, but we feel that many more remain to be found or discovered, and that they will be gained through science rather than through philosophies that deal only with abstractions or with the past."

"Yes, I agree with you that essentialism does have a philosophical base," said Reed, "even if it is not the same base as the perennialist, but I would still like to know what the ramifications of this philosophy are for educational practice."

"I probably tend to avoid your question because I think the answer is somewhat implicit in what I have already said," replied Estabrook. "However, I will try to be more explicit. We favor scientific investigation, and some essentialists are scientists, such as Conant and Rickover. We think that the facts of science should be made available to people on all levels of schooling. We would also like to encourage students to investigate things themselves, and to do it with objectivity. What I mean by this is not to be led astray by elaborate ideologies, no matter how persuasive they may seem to be. We like creative thinking, even philosophical thinking, but we think it should be erected as much as possible upon the facts we have already discovered about the universe. We don't think much of philosophies or religions that ignore what data we have discovered through long and tedious investigations about the universe. We think that students should have a solid grounding in things like biology, chemistry, astronomy, and the other sciences. We think they should know about the past by reading history, but it should be a history which also deals with facts rather than the editorializing or wish-fulfillment of the historian. We are not opposed to people wishing or dreaming, but we think they should know that they are wishing or dreaming when they do so. We would like to see educators become more hard-headed about teaching the really important things of the universe and making certain that all students have this. We don't like to go into schools and find students encouraged to discuss things that they have no foundation for discussing. If man is to move ahead he must move ahead from a solid base of knowledge, and it is this kind of base that we should like to see the schools form in the life of each and every individual."

"I wish to thank the essentialist," said Price, "for clearing so much ground for me. As you are well aware, we consider progressivism to be a scientific philosophy, and if the essentialist is not too chagrined, I would like to say that the scientific roots he mentioned are certainly ones that we also like to think led historically to the development of pragmatism, and which in turn implied a 'progressive' philosophy of education. We feel, however, that as important and as useful as scientific discoveries and facts have been, that scientists have neglected a very important side of science, and that is the application of science and particularly the scientific method, to the social, political, and educational problems of society. The work of Charles Sanders Pierce and William James was instrumental in making scientific method more meaningful in our everyday lives, and both certainly saw the reciprocity that should exist between science and philosophy which was also mentioned by the essentialist. Both Pierce and James spoke of science as a discipline which put ideas to work and believed that the truth or falsity of an idea was based on just how well it worked when it was tested. Since metaphysical questions such as 'Is there a God?' or 'How many angels can stand on the head of a pin?' cannot be tested in any empirical way, they are, from the pragmatist's point of view, pseudo-problems. They remain, at best, as hypotheses. I think one can readily see that the pragmatist has delimited inquiry to ideas that can be used in some way or other, and it was James who talked about the 'cash value' of ideas. James felt that we should only deal with questions whose answers might result in some real use. Thus, even if one could know the answer as to how many angels could sit on the head of a pin, whether it be forty thin ones, or three fat ones, such an answer would only have academic use. It would, we might say, bake no bread. It just would not be a useful answer in the day-to-day world in which we live. Answers to such questions as 'How can we stop pollution?' 'How can I find a better job?' and 'What should I do with my life?', however, are all questions worth asking, whose answers have cash value by enriching and improving our lives. This idea of work, however, as James pointed out, is interpreted by 'tender-minded' people as working to enrich their lives poetically and emotionally, whereas the 'tough-minded' person is looking for those ideas which are true by all observable scientific standards. The idea of religion, for example, might work in making some people feel more secure, but in terms of any scientific test of validity there would be no way of testing whether or not it was actually true. Basically, however, James believed that things that worked were true and things that did not work were false."

"Which leads to a relative concept of truth," interrupted Pennington.

"Yes, that's correct. Things are true only when they work and only in so long as they continue to work. They are false when they do not. This means that a thing may work and be true, and then stop working, and become false. Let me give you an example of what I mean. One way that has been utilized for keeping peace between nations was the use of power politics and a show of might. One might recall Theodore Roosevelt's 'great white fleet' and argue that this worked for a number of years. But in today's world of nuclear armaments where even a small country might have a weapon large enough to wipe out a country many times its size, the effect of a big country's pressuring a small one is no longer as effective as it once was. Power politics, if it ever was effective, no longer works and is therefore false as a political strategem. It is like saying that a hand plow once worked for clearing and cultivating land, but it no longer works as effectively as a tractor for this purpose. If we were to put this in the form of a question we might say, 'Is it true that the tractor is a better clearer and cultivator of land?' and the answer would be yes. We might say that the method of instruction used in the Middle Ages whereby students copied down every word of the text was a workable method in its time, but it is no longer as workable in that such texts can be readily and inexpensively produced. Thus, to the question 'Was this a workable method at the time?' we might answer 'True.' But in today's terms it would be 'False.' However, I wish to point out that any conception of what is true or false is only accepted tentatively, or with 'warranted assertibility.' Things that are false may later become true or vice-versa."

"I don't want to argue with you basically," said Estabrook, "because I think we are all pragmatists to some extent, but don't you believe some things are more reliable than other things?"

"Yes, that's true. Some things we put a great deal of faith in because they work over and over. But we must be aware that length of time is not a good criterion for maintaining such faith *ad infinitum*. We have to learn to scrap old and cherished ideas when they stop working."

"You haven't mentioned John Dewey," said Beattie.

"I was coming to him. John Dewey, as you are all well aware, was a pragmatist. What Dewey did was to utilize the pragmatic approach in dealing with social problems, and in particular, education. The essentialist says that we are all pragmatists, and I agree that most of us consider ourselves as pragmatists, for who would admit to doing things that don't work? But I think that when you really look at it you see that although people consider themselves pragmatic they are not pragmatic in their actions. Now, you might well ask why people persist in doing things that don't work, and I will tell you. Primarily, it is due to such things as custom and tradition. Dewey found that in education there were many things being done only because they had already been done, or because people were fearful of change. Dewey challenged the rote lock-step method of education in this country and, as you know, opened up the Laboratory School at the University of Chicago which was to meet the pragmatic test of helping children to learn better and to develop whatever potentiality they had for a decent aesthetic, social, and physical existence."

"The 'whole-child' concept," stated Reed.

"Yes, that's right. Dewey saw the application of scientific method in much broader terms than the essentialist suggests. He saw it as pervading a person's whole life, that people should be concerned with making their lives work better, and they can only do this by learning how to solve problems. Therefore, the development of problem-solving ability, which is really what the scientific method is, became an essential part of what was called progressive education."

"Just for the record," said Reed, "could you give us a rundown of just what this problem-solving method consists of?"

"Yes, of course. I'll paraphrase Dewey in this if you don't mind. He believed that all thinking began with a problem. The first step, therefore, is to find out whether it is a real problem or a pseudo-problem. If it is a real problem whose answer would have cash-value or some meaning to our lives, we next state possible hypotheses for solving the problem. After that, we try one or more of the hypotheses, until we find one that works. If it works, then it is the true answer for that problem. If it does not work, it is false. If it has not been tested, then it is neither true nor false. Let me give you an example. If someone becomes lost while on a hunting trip, then we would say he has a real problem whose answer needs to be found as quickly as possible. He states possible alternatives: shouting for help, climbing a tree, building a fire, and so on. If he tries climbing a tree and it doesn't work, then it is false as an answer to that problem. If he builds a fire and someone sees it and rescues him then that was a workable hypothesis, and therefore a true answer to the problem. Since he did not shout we cannot say whether that would have worked or not, and so it is neither true nor false."

"I would like you to specify," said Beattie, "just why you think it is so important that people, including children, learn this problem-solving method."

"Yes, that's the crucial thing. I'll put it this way. We feel that it is important because we don't know what kinds of problems students are going to face when they get out of school, but we do know that they will face problems. Although the facts that Estabrook wants to teach them may be useful, they may not be because changing conditions often necessitate new kinds of facts. We know, for example, that most high school students will have to face the problems of getting a job, marriage, college, social relationships, and possibly military service. We do not know how much the world will change during the four years they are in college, i.e., the facts of existence, but we do think that problems will remain, and that knowing how to solve problems effectively and efficiently is the best safeguard we can give a student to ensure that his or her life will be lived with intelligence and happiness."

"The progressivist thanked the essentialist for breaking ground for him, but I must equally thank the progressivist for doing the same for me," said Reed. "Our root is pragmatism too, and we subscribe to all of those things the progressivist is in favor of such as problem-solving, child centeredness, school and community relationships, etc. Our contention, however, is that this useful method of problem-solving has been more utilized toward helping people solve problems related to their adjustment to society than to changing it. We can understand, for example, that when progressivism was at its peak, in the early 1900s, that there was a need for education to assist in the adjustment of thousands of immigrants to the American system as it then existed. But that day is over, and we feel that the real need in the United States at the present time is the kind of educational philosophy like reconstructionism that will help us to solve some of the major crises we are now experiencing. We live in a world where there is war, hunger, and racism, and we find that education is not being utilized in ways that help us to deal effectively with such problems. But let me stop here and say that the idea of using education as a way of encouraging and suggesting change is not a new one in the history of mankind. Plato, who has already been mentioned, was certainly a champion of change, as were many of the other Greeks. Not only did they champion change in general but also moved toward the kinds of goals that reconstructionists believe in. The Stoics, for example, extolled the idea of world citizenship which is something that most reconstructionists would support. There have been various Chinese philosophers such as Tao, who in 1933 organized the Chinese Association for Promoting Universal Education, which aimed at the national reconstruction of education in China. In addition to these there have been numerous utopian writers from

Plato on down who promoted, in one way or another, ways to reconstruct education; thinkers such as More, Andreae, Gott, Campanella, Owen, Butler, Bellamy, Morris, Cram, and Wells. All of these writers suggested ways of changing education for the future. Reconstructionists have often been accused of being more concerned with the future than the present, but this is an overstatement. We would like to see many changes made in the present, changes that would provide better housing, an end to discrimination and hostilities between people and nations, an end to poverty, and so on. But we do feel that these changes, as necessary as they are, should be made in terms of some far-reaching and thought-out plan. To deal with such problems as if they were unrelated to other problems in the universe, or in a narrow time-sequence, only causes the problems to reappear over and over again. We want to solve these problems, but we would like to solve them in ways that solve them once and for all, and prevent their reappearance at a later date, and often in a worse form. In education, as well as in the various social areas I mentioned, reconstructionists would like to see greater planning with greater commitment to the need for education at all levels of society. We think that commitment to education should be total, and that state and national governments should be very much involved in planning for education not only for the world of the present, but also for the world of the future."

"But how can we do that when we don't know what the future will be?" asked Pennington.

"That's true. We can't know for sure. But we must learn to anticipate, and further than that, we think that man must take a very positive role in shaping the future, and that education can be a very vital force in this respect. We reject the notion that the future is something that just happens to people. It happens because certain things are put into effect, so that the future is not this random thing that most people conceive it to be. It is interesting to find in *Men Like Gods* by H. G. Wells, for example, that the educators have taken such a position and are in the vanguard of those who are directing social change."

"I'm afraid that the public at present is not ready for the idea of the educator as leader," said Extan.

"Yes, I feel that we are rather treated as servants," replied Reed, "and that is how most of the public pictures us. But in a way we deserve such an image because we have always acted as servants. Reconstructionists think that teachers have a moral obligation to use what they have learned for the betterment of society, and that not to use such knowledge is to act immorally."

"You are really saying, then, that not to act may be immoral."

"Very definitely, just as it was immoral for Germans not to act when Jews were being taken by the trainloads through their sleepy towns to the gas chambers."

"Would you advocate unionism for teachers in this respect," asked Estabrook, "or even perhaps more militant action on the part of teachers?"

"We feel that unions have played a very vital part not only in advancing the rights of miners, automobile workers, and railroad men, but also teachers. I would say that many reconstructionists support the idea of unionism, and many are union members. As to more militant action, we have no absolute answer here. It would depend on the situation. We do not, however, rule out the possibility of militant action, even very strong militant action."

"Just for the record," said Price, "I would like to point out that Dewey was also a strong advocate of unionism among teachers, as have been many progressivists."

"Yes, I realize that," replied Reed. "We applaud him for his action in that respect. Our quarrel with progressivism is not so much with Dewey as it is with some of his followers who we feel attempted to water progressivism down to the point where it was no longer a useful social philosophy. It is interesting to note that Dewey himself left the Progressive Education Association because he felt it was not championing the ideas of progressivism as he saw it. But if I may proceed further, I cannot fail to mention two contemporary thinkers who have done a great deal to advance reconstructionism as an educational philosophy, and these two men are George Counts and Theodore Brameld. Counts, in a number of writings, suggested that educators become involved in social affairs, that they even run for public office, and that they become heard on various social issues. The idea has always been a stimulating one, but I am afraid that not many teachers have followed Count's advice, and perhaps for good reason, for those teachers who have been involved in political or social causes have run into a great deal of conflict with educational administrators, legislators, the public press, and the public as well. I think it is the view of most people, in education and out, that teachers should stick to their classrooms and leave the problems of the world to others. Counts, in his essay entitled *Dare the School Build a New Social Order?* said that teachers should try to build a better world, but that idea has not attracted a wide following among educators. There is an organization devoted to this idea called the Society for Educational Reconstruction,[2] but they have only been in existence for a short time. Theodore Brameld is another educator who in a number of books and articles has championed the need for educators to become social activists at all levels of school and society. Brameld has strongly endorsed the idea of the school giving young people an awareness of social problems, as well as the actual experience of being involved in community projects. He has suggested that the teachers and the schools spend considerably more time outside the classroom with students learning subject matter by actually participating in the use of it. Engineering might, for example, be taught in one of the local factories, journalism at the newspaper office, and cooking at the local restaurant. As you can see, reconstructionists still feel that education is too much of an ivory-tower affair, and even though progressivists suggest 'learning by doing,' it is still a game played in the classroom rather than in the arena of life."

After a pause the existentialist said: "Yes, that is a very ringing refrain. Probably more than any other educational philosophy we find sympathy with what you are trying to do, but we do have some points of contention that we would like you to ponder. Before stating what these might be specifically, however, let me, like the rest of you, try to establish just what the roots of our beliefs are, as well as how we arrived at them. To begin with, we are considered a contemporary philosophy, and perhaps we are in the sense that more has been written about existentialism in the last few years than ever before. But, historically, we go back at least to the middle 1800s. It was Søren Kierkegaard, a Danish theologian, who began to put together some ideas he had about man and society that started men thinking in a new direction. Kierkegaard was quite disturbed at how technology, mass communication, mass education, and all the rest, had eclipsed man and made him a slave to ideology, systems, and corporate profits. His ideas remained dormant until the middle 1900s when the effect of World War II turned the attention of German and French thinkers, particularly, toward a reevaluation of traditional values. One can understand, I think, how Germans and Frenchmen felt about a war which seemed to make previous ideas about patriotism, God, and brotherhood somewhat obsolete. In Germany there was Heidegger and Jaspers. In France there was Camus, Simone de Beau-

---

[2]Society for Educational Reconstruction, College of Education, University of Bridgeport, Bridgeport, Conn.

voir, and Jean-Paul Sartre. Both Sartre and Camus worked for the French underground newspaper *Combat,* and in a number of later plays and writings examined ideas about cowardice, commitment, and death. Although existentialists are in general agreement regarding their concern for the individual, there are mainly two basic divisions of existentialism: theistic and atheistic. Into the first division would go Kierkegaard and Tillich as Protestant theologians, Gabriel Marcel as Catholic, and Martin Buber as a Jewish existential theologian. Into the second camp could be put Nietzsche, Heidegger, Sartre, Beauvoir, and Camus. By far the leading work in existentialism has been done in France, and its primary spokesman is Sartre. When people discuss existentialism it is usually talked about in terms of Sartrian existentialism. In the United States the two leading proponents of existentialism in education, George Kneller and Van Cleve Morris, both deal with existentialism from a Sartrian point of view."

"Could you comment on the fact that many of the existentialists, Sartre in particular," said Reed, "write a great deal of material that is fiction?"

"Yes, I would be happy to," replied Extan. "As you are aware, both Sartre and Camus won Nobel Prizes for their writing, Camus in 1957 and Sartre in 1964. Both were quite prolific writers of fiction and non-fiction. One might include Simone de Beauvoir in this category also. I would say that the reason for the great work they have done in the arts field stems from two primary reasons. One is that they have seen the fiction-market, as well as the theatre, as ways to get their ideas over to a large segment of the general public, and secondly, many existentialists feel that since their ideas deal with 'action' rather than 'contemplation,' they are, therefore, best expressed in a medium that lends itself to action, i.e., the theatre, or fiction. If I might comment on one play, *No Exit* by Sartre, we see the story of three people who are trapped in a hotel room which turns out to be hell. The group consists of a coward, a lesbian, and a nymphomaniac, who spend their time torturing each other. 'Hell is other people,' has been an oft-quoted line from this play."

"Yes, I wanted to ask you about that," said Pennington. "Why is it that the existentialists spend so much time dealing with depravity instead of presenting their ideas in straight-forward philosophical writings?"

"They deal with it because it exists," replied Extan. "I think you see in all of existential literature a great attempt to be realistic. Think of all the novels you've read, and I would like to ask you in how many does the author present any of the characters having stomach pains, heartburn, going to the bathroom, and other such things? What Sartre and others have attempted to do is to make their writings reflect life, and you find people in their stories and plays who do all these things, as indeed we do in real life."

"I have heard it said that existentialism is not so much a philosophy as it is a way of life, like Taoism," said Beattie. "Would you comment on that?"

"I think it is a legitimate philosophy," said Extan, "but it is true that the emphasis is away from dreamy abstractions about how life should be and how one should live it. Existentialism puts its emphasis on action in the here-and-now, and it evaluates people on their commitment to action."

"All this action and doing sounds a bit like what the progressivist was promoting," said Estabrook.

"There is quite a difference," answered Extan. "We are not so concerned with consequences as he is. I mean that a thing might not work in pragmatic terms and it might still be the right thing to do. Camus talks, for example, about the Myth of Sisyphus where Sisyphus is condemned to roll a heavy stone up a steep mountain each day. It never works in the sense of getting him free, and he is destroyed by it in the end, and yet there is something noble about him continuing to engage in this task, even though it does not provide any solution to his problem. When you compare this to our own lives I think it points out that there is some value to being committed and engaged in things which might not work in terms of the values held by most people, and yet is something noble because of the dedication and intensity of the participant."

"The thing that bothers me so much," said Reed, "is that although I certainly like the idea of commitment and dedication, I feel that it is often so randomly engaged in. I mean it is nice to know that some people would feel so strongly about something that they would throw themselves under a tank, but shouldn't there be some concerted plan where their actions led to something of real value?"

"Who is to say that this is not an action of real value?" replied Extan. "It certainly may be to the one who performed it. As to your idea of a plan, we are quite skeptical of plans which in reality become ways of other-directing people. We don't see anything wrong with looking ahead and trying to make what one does as meaningful as possible, but we object to making people fit a plan. One of the great divisions between Camus and Sartre was this issue of existentialism versus communism. Can one be both communist and an existentialist? The problem is still with us and there are varying views, but the attempt to relate individual action to an ideology or a plan or a system is not a simple one to deal with, and it depends a great deal on the individual involved."

"What about the use of science?" asked Beattie. "Why are existentialists so opposed to science?"

"We are not necessarily opposed to science," replied Extan. "We just feel that science, predominantly technology, has been used extensively to belittle man, to engage him in wars for various ulterior motives, and to harm him physically. We would like to humanize science and technology, and make it more responsive to man as man, and not man as a machine. We fear that in education, as in other areas, we are beginning to treat man more and more as a robot and that he is beginning to actually respond that way. We want more freedom for man, the kind of freedom in education, for example, that exists at Summerhill. We would like to see this become pervasive throughout society, but we are not overly optimistic about this happening."

"Indeed, I think of existentialism as a somewhat pessimistic philosophy in general," said Price.

"It is not pessimistic, it is realistic. It deals with things as they are, and naturally, that sometimes means that we will be engaged in, or deal with things that are unpleasant. But because we do not like them, or because we are afraid of them, such as death, pain, suffering, etc., does not mean that they should not be explored. We also react strongly against simplistic or pat answers to problems. We do not think that any great utopian world will be found where all problems will be solved. Man, because he is man, will always have problems."

"This does seem like a suitable place for me to begin," said Beattie, "with this idea that man must always have problems. It is just such an attitude as this that we feel engenders problems. We think that man will always have problems, but they will be different ones, because the problems of today, the problems of hunger, disease, and perhaps even old age, will be eliminated. But let me go back and start at the beginning. It was interesting to hear, for example, how the essentialist, the pragmatist, and the reconstructionist, are so enamored of science, but then fail to pursue science to its fullest lengths. They like the method of science but they don't always like it when it creates 'disturbing' things, and they begin to withdraw back to what one might call 'the good old days of science.' We behavioral engineers certainly support the method of science, and we are equally indebted to those heroic scientists who prepared the groundwork for later things to come. And later things did come, and will always come. Our science, the science that began behavioral engineering, started with Pavlov. It was Pavlov who found that a dog could be conditioned by the sound of a bell to expect food. Eventually, we found that every animal could be conditioned in one way or another, and experiments have been done with squid, cats, birds, rats, etc. Some of these conditioning experiments have been quite complex, and rats have been conditioned to run mazes or to work cooperatively, pigeons have been taught to play ping-pong or to be aggressive, monkeys to press various bars, levers, and buttons. Conditioning has also been used by military research, and dogs have been conditioned to blow up tanks, and porpoises to blow up ships. I am not making any value judgment at this point about whether this is good or bad, I am simply stating that it can be done."

"Yes, and I am afraid that they are still doing it," said Price.

"There have also been many experiments with humans, and we find humans no more difficult to condition than any other animal, and certainly capable of doing much more than any other animal can. It was J. B. Watson who found that you could condition a child to hate dogs, cats, and other furry animals by presenting something furry to the child and accompanying it with punishment such as the sound of loud sirens or electric shock. It was also possible to decondition the child to love furry animals by presenting the animal in a reward situation where the child is presented with furry material while his mother holds him, or while he eats. There have been many others who advanced the use of conditioning," said Beattie, "but the man most responsible for the development of conditioning as it is used today is B. F. Skinner. Skinner's work with pigeons in the Skinner Box paved the way for much of the significant work that was to follow. What Skinner did was to reward pigeons consistently when they accomplished a specific task. He found that he could condition them to peck geometric designs, make turns, and even read words. Similar things were then done with other animals. I should like to point out that Skinner found no need for punishment or what we call aversive stimuli. Reward, or what is better referred to as 'reinforcement,' is enough to create the desired behavior we want. These experiments provided the basis for further experiments with people, and people have been conditioned to become aggressive, to move in particular ways, to say certain words, and to sleep in a certain pattern."

"What's the difference between conditioning and hypnotism?" asked Reed.

"There probably isn't as much as we are led to think. Hypnotism is most likely a kind of conditioning, but it generally deals with a lower level of consciousness. Although one might not know he is conditioned, he still operates as a conscious subject. I should like to point out, too, that just as hypnotism can be used to control breathing, the pulse, and body temperature, so, too, can we do the same thing through conditioning. Now, we might ask what is to be used to condition people? We use rewards such as money or praise. People are, as I know you are aware, already conditioned to a great extent by these things, but often the conditioning is random and not always reinforced immediately or consistently. Advertisers, for example, attempt to condition people to buy a certain kind of car, or a certain kind of food product by relating it to sex, springtime, or some other enjoyable thought. Politicians try to get you to vote by raising such good things in your mind as peace, prosperity, or a 'chicken in every pot.' The case is no different in education, and we have been conditioning students ever since education began, though I must say we have been guilty of using aversive conditioning more than positive conditioning. But children can be conditioned equally to study hard, to be polite, and all the other things we want through the use of grades, a teacher's smile or compliment, and even more tangible things like stars and diplomas. We certainly promote the use of conditioning in education but we find the greatest problem to be a lack of immediate reinforcement. What I am saying is that when a teacher gives a spelling test, for example, it is usually such a long time before she returns it that the children have lost any interest in the correct spelling of the words. They were greatly interested when they took the test, but by the time it comes back it is meaningless. This is similar to rewarding or punishing a dog three days after he jumps or fails to jump through a hoop."

"But you must be realistic," said Pennington. "It is very difficult for a teacher to give instantaneous rewards with the size classes they have, the bulk of assignments, and so on."

"I realize the difficulty," said Beattie, "but it must be done if we really hope to educate people. Class sizes can be reduced. Assignments can be machine-graded. And teachers can learn how to become more effective as conditioning agents. There is some hope already that this is being done, and one great step forward, I think, has been the development of teaching machines. Here you have a mechanism which is a very effective conditioner. The program in the machine is carefully prepared so that the learner can learn it in very small steps, and at each step he is rewarded, the reward being, of course, that he knows he got the right answer. When these machines were first produced, some rewarded children with bubble gum or even with spoken words, but we discovered that simply knowing that the answer is correct is enough reward to ensure that the student will remember the answer and be motivated to go on to the next question. We have found that students like to work such machines, and that they learn a great deal from them."

"I am raising this question only to have it clarified in my own mind," said Reed. "Will these machines delimit the number of teachers we have?"

"That is a recurring bugaboo among teachers," replied Beattie, "and my answer is no. I think that it will allow the teacher to deal with—and I think this should be of great interest to everyone here —a more philosophical approach to knowledge, as well as the more creative aspects of learning. If we can be assured that the machine will teach the facts of history, then the teacher can deal with the values and interpretation of those facts. We think that education historically has been conducted along essentialistic lines, and if it is to be continued this way to any extent, that machines can do this kind of job better than people can."

"You are saying that machines can do our job for us, is that it?" asked Estabrook.

"If education is to be looked upon in a fact-getting sense, yes," replied Beattie.

"Well, we don't deal with facts in such a matter-of-fact way as you think. We deal with values and interpretations too, but they are all intertwined. We certainly do not object to the use of machine learning. We are greatly in favor of it. We have no vested interest to protect. If machines can teach facts better than people can, then they should be used for that purpose."

"But what bothers me," said Pennington, "is that people are so machine-like already. Won't this just increase the problem? I hate to think of students relating to their machines."

"There is that danger here," said Beattie, "but I think that if we use our technology humanistically, and if we change the role of the teacher to be the kind of partnership role that the existentialist stresses, then machines will actually be a change for the better in education."

"The history of technological development has not led us to believe this will happen," said Extan. "When Nobel invented dynamite he had great hopes for its humanistic use in building canals and removing mountains, but as we have seen, it has largely been used to kill people. We feel that the use of conditioning, or 'behavioral engineering,' as you call it, has great potential harm for brainwashing people, and we are fearful that it will be used to indoctrinate much more than to educate."

"These are problems we must deal with," said Beattie. "But we must not turn our back on the enormous prospects that behavioral engineering offers for education, and in turn, for the advancement of mankind."

Questions for Discussion

1. Can you think of any other examples to support Pennington's statement that some of the ideas created a long time ago are more relevant to today's problems than ideas that were created yesterday? (p. 62)

2. In reference to the argument between Estabrook and Pennington (pp. 62–64), do you feel that ideas are material or immaterial? What support can you provide for your view?

3. How would you respond to the implication made by Estabrook that students are encouraged to discuss things they have no foundation for discussing? (p. 65)

4. Do you agree with the progressivist that knowing how to solve problems is the best safeguard we can give a student to ensure that his life will be lived with intelligence and happiness? (p. 69)

5. Can you think of any other ways that education might be done effectively outside the classroom in addition to the examples given by Reed? (p. 72)

6. Comment on Extan's criticism of the pragmatic notion of workability. (pp. 74–75)

7. Would you agree with Beattie that education has dealt more with aversive than positive conditioning? (p. 77) Give examples to support your view.

8. What do you think of the statement by the behavioral engineer that education has, historically, been largely conducted along essentialistic lines? (p. 78)

9. Comment on Pennington's view that machines may make people more machine-like. (p. 78)

4

The Fourth Day

As soon as the philosophers had seated themselves around the table, Pennington made a motion to be heard. "I would like," he said, "to deal more fully with the arguments presented during the last three days by the existentialist and the behavioral engineer; perhaps more the behavioral engineer since we feel that the existentialist does want to preserve something that is human, though I tend to think he wants to preserve what is animal more. It might help if I referred back to Aristotle to make my point. Aristotle, as you know, talked about man's vegetative nature, his animal nature, and his spiritual nature. We don't deny these exist. As a matter of fact we believe that the history of mankind has really been one where the vegetative side, that is, man's inertia and laziness, and his animal side, his aggressive instincts, have largely been in control. But because they have for so long is no reason, from our view, why they should be perpetuated. We do see a kind of struggle here for dominance, but we see no reason why these forces, as strong as they are, should be victorious. We are fighting for man's mind. We think that the spiritual side of man, though shunted and slighted by society, should reassert its mastery over man's existence and be in control. This would mean, as we see it, that man would be guided by reason instead of the other forces, as natural as they seem, which are seeking to satisfy their own desires. The battle is an uphill one. Ever since man became man, and that was at the point where he acquired reason, man has had to struggle with the forces that have tried to take over his soul. We feel that religion, however nonsensical it has been at times, has at least placed its emphasis in the right direction, that is, upon saving man's soul. Plato, as you know, is always talking about saving the soul, and that is what we feel one should do. But to save the soul, to make it grow, requires nourishment. That nourishment is ideas. We are not neglecting man's vegetative and animalistic side, but we think that a sort of balance should be created between competing forces, and that this balance can be achieved through man using his reason. I think that if we are honest with ourselves we do see that man makes reason paramount even though he is always complaining about it. It is true that reason is sometimes in error. It is true that reason sometimes asks us to do things that our body does not want to do. But when we look at the history of mankind, at the wars, or the maintenance of bad values, we see that the golden times of mankind were those times when man utilized his reasoning powers to create good governments or to create great works of art. We feel that man can continue to develop his reasoning powers to higher and higher states, but unfortunately, we are again living in a kind of Dionysian period where people are extolling body over mind. We see this attitude, for example, in the trend toward sensitivity training, toward great concern for grooming, clothing, and all the other things that cater to man's fleshly desires. Imagine, if you will, how far we could go if man gave half as much attention to the care of his mind as he does to his body. We feel that much of what passes for education today, instead of elevating man's mind, really lowers his mind to what his body wants. The behavioral engineer says that he will condition man to act in certain ways because he can do it. To this end he will utilize various rewards, such as money, praise, and so on. But what about man assisting in his own development? What about his own free choice to become conditioned or not to become conditioned? And what is the conditioning toward anyway? We don't want the kind of world that the conditioner is leading us toward. It would be much better, I think, if men lived a little hungry and a little less clad in clothing, but were immersed in great thoughts, yet, I do not see the behavioral engineer moving us in that direction. The world he is moving us toward is one of gadgetry and mechanical human beings. This kind of world leaves no room for spirit, for hope, for creativity. We don't want to be pushed into something even if it does seem to be for our own good, or even if most people want it. We want to emphasize the human and spiritual qualities of man, and not those qualities that lead him to satisfy what his body says it wants or needs. Although the existentialist disagrees with much of what the behavioral engineer is trying to do, we feel that his view of man is also limited and perhaps somewhat perverted. He wants to bring out the animal again, as if we hadn't seen enough of that. We have had the animal in control of man for many years, and it has been to our detriment. We want a man of reason, a man who can rise to the kind of heights that are worthy of him. Although, as you can see, I have deliberately tried not to mention the religious aspect, I cannot really continue to do so. Let us look at it this way. If there is a supreme being, or spiritual power, then there are in the world higher forces. Further, if these powers created man then they may serve as models for man. So that as man moves toward these spiritual powers in terms of using his ideas he is also becoming more spiritualized. That is what we are after, the spiritualization of man, and we reject those philosophies that for whatever reason are trying to bind man to the here and now, and we find all of you guilty of that in some respect. I do agree that this demands a certain attitude about man that might not be provable in your terms. But we think that this view, rightly or wrongly, serves to give us something that is uplifting and holy. We do not like to think that we must deal with man as an animal or a machine, but as a creature possessed of unlimited spiritual powers."

"I'm afraid," said Extan, "that you do not see all the dangers that emanate from your view. It is precisely because people dealt with man as something beyond man that we got into all the trouble in the first place. You keep mentioning the religious aspect, and yet history shows that men who were immersed in ideas, and were intellectuals primarily, were no less prone to war, violence, or inhumanity, than those who were not. I am always reminded in this respect of the priest in Victor Hugo's *Nôtre Dame de Paris,* who was the arch villain and rightly so, even though he paraded under the cloak of intellect and morality."

"You also mentioned," said Beattie, "that there was very little tangible proof for your position, and with that I agree. I know of no real evidence that man has this spiritual side you keep talking about, or that he has ever had it. I can give you plenty of proof that he has a brain, a heart, and so on. Your views are really based on a kind of dreamy abstractionism that I find impossible to accept."

"You expect tangible proofs for some things, but not for others," answered Pennington. "And yet all of us live lives that are not based on proofs. I mean we all love, and yet no one has even seen it, or weighed it, or measured it. We all believe in justice, and yet one cannot see it under a microscope. Our lives are filled with abstractions and I think our lives are so much the better because of them."

"It is true that we can't measure love per se, or see justice," said Beattie, "but we can arrange conditions so that love will occur, or so that men will be just, without resorting to abstractions at all."

"One might also say," said Price, "that we can in a sense measure love or justice in terms of their consequences."

"I disagree," said Pennington. "To measure something in terms of its consequences is not to measure it at all. It is just that you are unwilling, or say that you are unwilling, to accept things that you can't measure, and yet I contend that you do so every day. And when we look at what has enriched man's life the most—love, beauty, wisdom—we find that they are things quite outside the realm of the kind of materialism you promote. They are measurable only in terms of the kind of inspiration they give to mankind."

"Yes, we know all about inspiration," replied the progressivist, "only we call it motivation. Though we question seriously what you want to motivate them toward, or against."

"I think I've talked enough about 'for,' " said Pennington. "Let me say what I would motivate them against. To begin with, we do not like studies that only deal with everyday affairs. If they do, they should deal with them in ways that are more uplifting. We think that philosophy and religion should have a place in every study. We are also opposed to specialization in the narrow sense of that word. We prefer studies that deal with issues in a broader and more unified sense. We are, of course, opposed to the kind of triteness and hackneyed ritual we find in education, and we certainly want a higher quality of work. We don't think that technology is the entire answer to man's development, and we want him to take an interest in his own development in a very real sense. We want him, in a word, to become more holy."

"If I may interject," said Price. "I have been listening patiently to you for some time now, but I must strenuously object to a continuation of this kind of tender-mindedness. We must deal with reality as reality no matter what kind of romantic notions we might have to lead us on to other paths. The fact is that there are too many problems in the world that need to be solved without getting into areas that I might say are sport for academic thinkers. I think, for example, to promote the kind of ivory towerism which you do, or to deal with the kinds of pseudoproblems you do is quite immoral in a world where people need education to keep them from starving, or to gain basic skills, and to solve problems relating to their survival."

"I couldn't agree more," said Estabrook.

"Yes, with the only difference being," said Price, "that we see these problems solved through the use of problem-solving techniques, while you, Estabrook, see it through learning certain amounts of basic data that you would utilize in applying to such problems. But to continue with my objections to the perennialist, we feel that you have fostered another idea that has led man astray, and this is the idea that one should search for your kind of Platonic universals, the quest for certainty. We feel that this has been a very misleading kind of education and a rather futile quest in that such certainties most likely do not exist, and even if they did, would probably be of little use in helping man in his everyday activities. Plato attacks studies that deal with material things as studies that deal with illusion. Then he sets up illusions himself in telling man that he should pursue these eternal and perfect truths. I know of no such eternal truths man has found yet."

"What about mathematics," asked Pennington. "Don't you consider those truths absolute?"

"Not in the least," answered Price. "Such truths are only true in context, only analytically. Two plus two equals four simply means four equals four. Who would object to such a statement? No one, except on the grounds that it isn't really a meaningful statement at all. It is only a clarifying statement. Mathematicians and scientists do not find absolutes. Only philosophers claim that privilege. This problem was really heightened by Aristotle. The whole method of deductive reasoning encouraged man in the idea that he had hold of some absolutes and that through them he could get some more. The scientific view is more in the inductive vein, that is to say that from a number of observations we arrive at certain scientific laws."

"Then it's the same thing," said Pennington. "*We* start with laws and *you* end with them."

"Not at all," said Price. "The difference is that our laws are not absolutes whereas yours are. Ours are only probabilities, only things we accept with a certain 'warranted assertibility.' Take the law of gravity, for example. To us this only means that no circumstance has yet arisen to dispute such a law, though one could at any time. It is possible that through an atom bomb blast things could be so arranged that such a law would no longer apply. But when we take your axioms, or absolutes, such as 'God exists,' you cannot possibly see that as something which may be changed or abandoned at some future date."

"We feel that not only are there some things that don't change," said Pennington, "but that man is much better for believing so. It gives him a locus, a sense of permanence and stability."

"But at what cost?" asked the progressivist. "Although this may sound like a small matter, and I don't think it is, in most perennial schools that I have visited not only was the subject matter rather rigid, as well as the ways of teaching it, but you even had bolted-down seats. Certainly that would give the student a feeling for permanence. But when progressivism began to pick up steam as an influence on education in the twenties we took out that kind of bolted-down furniture and replaced it with movable desks and chairs. Our intent was to give the student some sense of change. We didn't want him to think of life as stationary and permanent like his chair had been. We also made the curriculum more flexible and the methods of teaching as well. Your call for permanence and stability, I feel, is really overcompensation for the feeling of insecurity that you have."

"If I might speak here," said Reed, "we find that there are a number of people afraid of change, and it probably is a personality problem as well as anything else. And because they cannot handle change, they reject it for everyone else."

"One thing that people should realize," said Price, "is that there cannot be any improvement without change. It is true that change could lead you the wrong way, but you still cannot hope to go anywhere without change."

"As much as I have argued against the perennialist," said Estabrook, "I am sympathetic to his trying to provide some kind of stable base for man to move from. There are a number of people who promote change and more change, but we find there is nothing in change itself which makes it necessarily a virtue. We are for change too, but we think change should come slowly and meaningfully. We don't feel that things are necessarily good because they are old, but neither are they necessarily good because they are new, and we know of teachers who pride themselves on always using the latest book or technique even though that book or technique does not work as well as the one rejected. Only recently did I have occasion to go through the educational shelves of a rather large university library, and I began to compare the educational texts written fifty years ago with those written today. I would say that the ones I saw written fifty years ago were much better than their contemporaries. We know, too, in education, how much we change things, only after long suffering and travail to change back to the way things were in the first place. We talk so much in education about innovation, and yet most of the innovations that work are things that we found worked a long time ago. We find some value in what the perennialist says about the classics, for example. We think that the classics are probably better for students to read than most of the things one finds on best-seller lists, though we do feel that modern books can be valuable too, even more valuable if carefully chosen. We think that there should be some sort of selectivity process going on in education, and that educators have renounced their responsibility to be judges of what is best. They leave it to the students to decide, and except for a few students, most choose things that could not be construed as educational in any possible sense. We think that there should be some standards set in education such as a standardized curriculum, standardized teaching certification, standardized methods of teaching, and so on. We would like to guarantee that every child, no matter what part of the country he lives in, could be assured of having a basic education. However, we find that 'progressive' approaches have so weakened education to the point that it is dramatically ineffective in providing children with even the rudiments of a good education. We would like to see the training of teachers upgraded, and we would like to see more dedication on the part of teachers toward teaching useful subject matter. Look at the case as it presently exists. People are being graduated from our schools who can barely read and write. I know of one case where a young person who, when called before a judge, informed him that he was a high school graduate. The judge disputed this, and the boy produced his high school diploma. When the judge asked the boy to read his diploma, however, he couldn't. This is the state we are in where we have social promotions, survey courses, appreciation courses, and all the other sorts of things that allow children to escape any concentrated effort to learn important things. There is, as you all know, a great state of permissivism in education. We are told that we should be child-centered. Look where this has led us. One cannot get decent music on the radio today because the young make all the standards. Not only in music, but in clothing, in art, and all the rest. Those who could set better standards are older and hence not listened to. Sadly enough, the educators have given lip service to the idea that the young should rule our schools, as if there were some fount of wisdom that the young were privy to that those over thirty are not. It is little wonder, therefore, that our schools have been turned into playpens where whatever one does is all right, and the less one does the better. Everyday we see the students gaining more control over what they do, so that everyday they do less and less. There are schools today where all one has to do is wait the required time and he graduates whether he does anything or not. All you have to do to find out how effective this approach can be is to talk to anyone who has to hire high school graduates and he will tell you how they can't write a decent sentence or add a column of figures, or don't want to work at all for that matter. It is true that the older schools made a fetish out of rote work and memorizing facts and all the rest, but in order to correct this problem it was not necessary to throw out all discipline, all work, all order, which has been done of late. We feel that students need to know what it is like to do something hard, to engage in the serious business of education, and to come out with some hard-core knowledge that one can apply in terms of one's work and life."

"I am not sure what you mean by challenging child-centeredness," said Price. "Does that mean that you support subject-centeredness?"

"This seems to be part of the problem I've seen in the thinking here," said Estabrook. "That is, that if you are against something, then that means that you are for the opposite. We respect the rights of people as individuals, and we would certainly like them to do things they are interested in, but we feel that there are limits, and that if a child wants to study basket weaving when he needs to know basic mathematics, we would insist that he study basic math and that after he learns this, then perhaps he could do basket weaving. But we are not so subject-oriented that we are going to always insist that the child not follow any of his own desires. We do feel that as one gets into the business of serious studying, that generally he begins to find it more and more appealing, and develops interests of his own which parallel those of his educators. But we have no assurance that the child has certain innate tendencies that insure that he will study the right things. We think there is a need for some direction in education and that the child looks to the adult for direction. It is only when he doesn't find it, or else finds the educators so lacking in any desirable qualities whatsoever, that he begins to turn inward to himself for direction."

"What's wrong with that?" asked Extan. "What he chooses himself he will be more involved in."

"Yes, but we don't often find him choosing things that he should be involved in," replied Estabrook. "We can see the art of tattooing as a possible area of interest, but we wonder that just because a child is interested in tattooing that he should be allowed to pursue it, or that an entire curriculum in tattooing should be set up just because he expresses some interest in it. We all know that there were certain subjects that we didn't want to study in school and would have gotten out of if we could, and yet, today, probably they are the most valuable things that we do know. Remember too, gentlemen, we are talking here, or at least I am talking about, school time. We are talking about what should be going on during those five hours, five days a week. We feel that these should be devoted to serious matters. The rest of the time, outside, you can do what you want—teach the child driver education, social dancing, home economics, or what have you. But let's not bring that sort of thing into the school and call it education."

"We would have been quite happy if the outside forces you mentioned had taken care of teaching those things adequately," Price responded. "I don't think any of those who call themselves progressivists really wanted the school to go into sex education, driver education, vocational training, or any of the rest. It was only that we found these things so necessary, and so poorly done, or else not done at all, that we had to get into it. We do not really see the school as separate from society as you do, and if these things are important to know, and are not being taught, then we feel that the school has to do it."

"We very definitely see the school as related to society," said Estabrook. "As a matter of fact we see it so related that we see the breakdown of our educational system as very definitely related to the breakdown of morals, marriage, patriotism, and religion. It is because students do not have to apply themselves, or work hard, that many of our present problems have arisen."

"I fail to see how teaching a standard curriculum like you suggest would solve our social problems," said Extan. "Perhaps you might expand on this a bit more."

"Yes, I'd be happy to," answered the essentialist. "Today, from the moment a child begins school, he is told that he's supposed to be happy, that there will not be much pressure put upon him, that he is as good as anyone else, and that if he is having problems it is not really his fault, and he should see a counselor, or the school psychiatrist, or someone else, to straighten out the matter. It is never his own fault that he does badly. Consequently, as a child goes through school he resents being judged, graded, or made to feel in any way that he can or needs to improve himself as a human being. So that by the time he finishes high school he is a person who feels superior without really knowing anything, is highly verbal, very much influenced by group attitudes, and now thinks he is ready to venture into life. When he does, however, he finds it quite different than what he experienced in high school. He finds that people do hold him responsible, that he must work hard, that there are some people who know more than he does, and that they are rewarded accordingly. He becomes frustrated and angry, but instead of blaming this on his educators and on the schools, he blames it upon society, or upon his wife and family, and out of this comes a great deal of hostility. Most, if not all, of those who call themselves hippies and anarchists are products, not of the kind of education I am promoting, but of the kind promoted by progressivism and existentialism. In terms of your own criteria of workability I think you can see that it is not working, and not only is education being destroyed, but society as well."

"I should like to interrupt here for a moment if I may," said Reed. "I am aware that the progressivist and the existentialist can answer for themselves, but I am not sure that I would think their answer would go far enough. I agree that life is not like it is in the schools, but I do not think that the changes you have suggested would bring it more in line with life, but rather less in line with it. What I think we find when we look at society is that it has undergone great changes and yet the schools are still teaching for and about society like it was. The schools have not kept up, are not keeping up, and are even falling further behind every day. Our contention is that instead of being a follower of social change, and a slow follower at that, the schools should be in the vanguard of change and actually fomenting change. I know that this idea rattles many in education and in society as well, but I seriously wonder why people in the educational profession, who should be in a leadership position in America, are so content to follow rather than to lead. Many innovative procedures are blocked by people in the profession of education who find it difficult to adjust to change, and who resent and are fearful of the schools establishing policies for the nation as a whole. We all know the image of the American teacher. He is cringing, fawning, anxious for any little crumb that the establishment throws at him, generally ready to protect the traditional values, and content to teach the ABC's, mathematics, and the other routine subjects. What we are calling for is a new breed of teacher, a teacher who will challenge, lead, disrupt, and create new values. Such a teacher will not only serve as a social innovator but as a model for his students to follow."

"It sounds like the prototype of a revolutionary," said Estabrook.

"Exactly," replied Reed. "Yes, the teacher will be a revolutionary; not a violent one, necessarily, but one who is working for the new social order that must come if we are to solve our present social dilemmas. When we look at the history of education we see that all of the great figures in education challenged the education of their time and wanted to change it. Plato wanted to change Athenian education, so did Aristotle. Rousseau was plainly against the education of his time, as was Dewey, Montessori, and anyone else you care to mention. Who, I ask you, defended the education of their time? I can tell you that it was the small thinkers. It was those without vision, without the creative spark. Unfortunately, the history of mankind is thought of only in terms of what man has done. Too often we overlook the great ideas which spurred such action, and which will further action in the future. Look at Plato—his ideas are still much in the future. Many have yet to be implemented, yet, I feel, will be at some future time, such as the control of marriage and the family, not to mention state control of the educational system. Look at Dewey. Although many of his ideas have been put into operation, many others still remain untried and futuristic. We want more goal-setting in education. We want more experimenting, even on a radical scale, and instead of this we get a cry which says hold the fort, we're moving too fast and we should go back to old ways. I realize that there are many people suffering from 'future shock,' from the great progress that has been made, but such future shock is largely from how society has changed and not education.[1] Education has not changed with the times, and is still refusing to change, or is at least succumbing to attempts to slow down change as much as possible. Carry this a step further and many people are afraid of education developing any kind of power base of its own. There are many people who are afraid of the idea of the school developing standards and values of its own which may propel people even further into differing mores, standards and programs. We feel that not to try new things, not to think ahead, is to court disaster, and that as Wells indicated, we are in a race between education and catastrophe. I know that I am being rather general. Let me now be more specific. What we hold dear in education today was once a radical idea. John Holt has remarked that 'Conservatism is the worship of dead radicals,' and with this I agree. The things that so many of you call the status quo were once revolutionary ideas, such as the idea of mass education, the idea of government support for education, the idea of teaching people to think for themselves, and many other ideas. We are opposed to education that supports the status quo because the status quo rapidly disintegrates into an acceptance of reactionaryism. We are also opposed to education that helps people to fit the system because we

---

[1]For further discussion concerning "future shock" see *Future Shock* by Alvin Toffler (New York: Random House, 1970).

think that the system should be changed. How many of you are satisfied with the way education is? None of you, really. Still, inadvertently you support the present system because you propose no alternative to it. And yet look at all of the things that could be improved in our society, and would be improved, if educators were to develop an attitude that said 'stop accepting and start proposing.' And I might add that it is very seldom that the innovative ideas in our society come from educators. It is very rare indeed. Usually they come from outside the educational establishment; only later, and after constant proof of their usefulness, do they become accepted in education. Why aren't educators the leaders of our society? Why, because they have seldom thought of themselves in that role, and it is daily that educators with ideas, with the courage to try something new, are threatened or fired from their positions. When we trace the development of any good idea in education, any good idea that even becomes implemented, we can trace it back to see the great number of individuals who were released from their jobs or intimidated because they supported that idea."

"I find," said Estabrook, "that instead of facing contemporary problems you always cop out by telling us how much better things will be in the future. I agree with you that there is a certain kind of personality that is always promoting futuristic solutions to contemporary problems, and that personality is primarily escapist in nature."

"That is just what I am not promoting," said Reed. "That would be to completely misconstrue my intent. What I am promoting are practical solutions to present problems, but I believe that practical solutions sometimes involve thinking outside of ordinary terms. This is to say that solving some contemporary problems may involve going further than people are generally accustomed to go."

"Although you've hinted around at certain societal changes," said Extan, "you've never come right out and said what these changes should be."

"I think that's true," said Reed, "but it is only because I have been fearful of speaking for all reconstructionists. Though we all feel the need for radical changes in the social structure, we do differ on what kind of changes are needed, and in what order. If you are asking me personally, however, what changes I would like to see, I will enumerate the following:

1)   all nations agree to an end of war as a way of settling international disputes and support all peace-keeping organizations such as the United Nations and the Bertrand Russell Peace Foundation

2) a national health service whereby all people receive free medical services, mental as well as physical

3) a cabinet position for education alone, with separate secretaries each for education, for health, and for welfare

4) unrestricted freedom of speech and press, the sole exception to be the deliberate telling of lies

5) support of the woman's liberation movement

6) support of all groups seeking useful ways to racially integrate our society

7) an end to compulsory schooling; children should have the right to attend or not attend school, and if children do not wish to take advantage of education as it presently exists, then society will have to change education in ways to make it more appealing

8) a tax structure that taxes more justly, and which distributes wealth in more equitable ways, limiting the income of individuals and corporations

9) an end to the seniority rule in Congress which allows older members to dominate and control committees; also, the establishment of a basic test for all candidates for political office, which gauges their knowledge of other nations, financial matters, I.Q., leadership and creative ability

10) greater use of the wealth of nations for improving the environment as well as educational and artistic endeavors

11) twenty-four hour day-care centers, staffed by professional educators, doctors, and nurses, where parents can leave their children free of charge for as long as they desire

"That is a rather comprehensive list," said Estabrook, "but I am sure that we could all compile a list of things we would like to see changed in society. I think one of the points that we might agree on is that none of us is satisfied with the way things are."

"Yes, I would be very interested in your doing that," said Reed. "Up until now we spoke about changes that one might make in the manner of education, but I think that if we search more deeply we all see that education and society are so tied together that to change one we must change the other.

"Yes, that's true," said Price, "I think we all see that. I would be happy to start it off if no one objects. To begin with, if one reads Dewey he knows that we progressivists have long been champions of the idea of bringing school and society together. It was for that reason that we promoted the idea of parent-teacher organizations, civic groups concerned with education, educating within the community structure, and utilizing community resources in the educational program. We saw the school as an agent for change in the community, while in turn recognizing that there were certain forces being exerted by the community which had their influence upon the school. As to the things we would like to see changed in society I shall enumerate a few. To begin with, we feel that society has long been dominated by a Puritan ethic which has greatly influenced education and made it despotic and cruel. This Puritan ethic, we feel, has been greatly supported by religious influences that have dominated education in Europe and the United States for centuries. While championing a pluralistic society where one may be free to worship as he likes, or to send his child to the school of his choice, we think that public schools should be kept free of the propagandizing that we find most religions promoting. Since religion is based largely on superstition and untestable hypotheses, we feel that it is not the same as other subjects in that it cannot be challenged, and is certainly not presented to students as other subjects are, but rather as something rather mystical and beyond reproach. I think you could say that progressivism has tried to be a force to uproot the religious tradition in American education and we have succeeded to some extent. However, the danger is ever-present, and we do find people sneaking religion back into education in many subtle ways. There are such things as released-time programs, a sharing of facilities between parochial and private schools, and outright financial aid to private schools by state and federal agencies. We shall continue to press for an end to any sort of religious studies except those presented as a sort of comparative religion course where the student would be free to question and reject."

"Yes, I was going to ask you about that," said Reed. "You would not then be opposed to teaching religion in the schools if it were done on an objective basis?"

"Not at all," replied Price. "In fact we would welcome it, provided it were done in ways that did not lead the student to think of it as something beyond analysis and suspicion."

"I am often afraid," said Pennington, "that those who say they are trying to get religion out of the school often substitute some dogmatic philosophy in its place, such as say progressivism."

"I don't think that is true," answered Price. "We are not dogmatic in the least. We are quite ready to change our methods or our views when they are no longer viable."

"You mean when they do not work," said Pennington.

"Yes, that's right," replied Price.

"That's what I mean," said the perennialist. "You are setting up workability as a dogmatic principle in education which becomes as unquestionably true as your claim that religion is."

"We do fail to see how doing things that do not work would be of any benefit," responded Price. "We think that everyone starts with certain assumptions. One of ours is that we should do things that work. We do not find religion working in the sense that it is helping to turn out the kinds of students we think we should be turning out. We find that religion encourages students to be dogmatic, undemocratic, and separatist. As to making workability into some kind of religion, that is simply not true. We accept the criterion of workability with recognition of its shortcomings and with the idea that it is only a method that will be discarded if better methods come along. But let me go on, for religion is not the only area of society that we feel needs to be considered for improvement. Another is the need we find on every hand to preserve the status quo. Needless to say, for all of those who feel that progressive education has been so successful, and that it has changed the mores of America, created juvenile delinquency, and the rest, I should like to point out that if we had really been successful we would have wiped out this kind of attitude that we find so prevalent in America today. What I am saying here is that most schools exist to promote and protect the status quo. Much of this, we feel, is the result of a business attitude toward our country and toward the school. We think that schools should not exist primarily for business purposes, but that it should be the other way around. We would like therefore, to see some change in the attitude which says that we should try to save what we have. If you know anything about progressivism at all, you know that we promote change in our political, business, and social structures. Such change occurs all too slowly, however, and we feel that schools are not doing their job in making people aware of the necessity of change."

"You are beginning to sound like the reconstructionist," said Extan.

"Yes, I suppose so. It is not that we are against change. Certainly we are for it, and I hope that I have helped to end that life-adjustment myth once and for all. However, I think a difference might be that we see change occurring gradually, perhaps even orderly, through a kind of evolutionary process, whereas the reconstructionist sees a more immediate and revolutionary kind of change."

"Yes, I would agree with your statement," replied Reed. "We do feel that your process takes a very long time. We think you are making some effect, but as you yourself admit, you don't really see that much progress in this direction."

"If I may be permitted to say so," said Extan. "I don't really see that much difference between the two of you. I mean, from my point of view you both believe in orderly change, whereas our point is that students must be radicalized to want change now. If I may be permitted also, I should like to say what *we* feel is wrong with society, and there are many things we object to. First of all, we object to the whole idea of any established system that must be supported or perpetuated, much less a system that dehumanizes and exploits people. We also object to religion, traditional religion that is, which is used to solace people and make them docile. We object to education that molds people for the system, and we object to the propagandizing we find in the public press, advertising, and throughout the mass media in general. We have no great belief that the schools as a system can correct these problems, but we do feel that individuals who are aware and concerned, can. We would like to hope that our educational systems would help to turn out such individuals, but to date we have not been greatly impressed with this as a possibility. We also object to the way people are taught to relate to each other through their schooling, the culture, and each other: that most people tend to treat each other as objects, as things to be manipulated for their own good, the good of the corporation, of society, or religion. We are, as you can see, against most of the values and institutions that most people hold so dear, and we have no great optimistic belief, as most of you seem to have, that education can correct all of the ills of either man or society."

"What you have said sounds completely nihilistic," said Estabrook. "It sounds very strange to me that you can find nothing good in contemporary society. I don't see how it could possibly be as bad as you say it is, and the only conclusion I can really come to is that your views are not based on anything objective, but rather on some psychological manifestation in your own personality which leads you to condemn and never to approve."

"I did not say that everything is to be condemned," replied Extan. "We feel that man is to be held responsible for what is good in the world as well as for what is evil. There have been good men, but unfortunately, as society shows, they were opposed by most other people. Socrates as well as Christ was put to death, Spinoza stabbed, Locke forced into exile, and so on. We feel that there is a great deal wrong, however, and a recent look at society has not been too encouraging. Let me go on, however, for there are other things that I object to. One of the things touched on by the progressivist, I feel was not brought out enough, and that is, who controls education, as well as the country? We agree that the country, as well as education, is controlled by big business. Look at your school boards. By and large, the people on your school boards are local businessmen: the heads of banks and small corporations, lawyers, doctors, etc. The same is true at the college level. Those who control our colleges, the trustees, are usually the heads of large corporations, or else those high in government positions. These people are, as has been pointed out here, and by numerous studies, ultraconservative. Yet, they make all of the high-level policies that govern education, and the reason it is so slow to change and so conservative is precisely related to who controls it."

"Who should control education then?" asked Beattie.

"The people," said Extan. "Particularly the people who go to schools or take part in them, that is to say, the faculty and the students. We are greatly opposed to control of education from the top by people who are really not a part of it. We would like to see local control of education from kindergarten through college."

"I am afraid I must disagree seriously with you," said Price. "I believe that your position is inspired by the most noble motives, but I am afraid that you do not see what the results of such a position would be. To begin with, we have had local control of schools in this country for quite some time. Our schools are still controlled by cities, states, or counties, and school systems may vary radically from city to city or county to county. We feel that to promote this still further would allow the schools to become instruments for local community prejudices and would result in a hodge-podge of methods and aims. We feel that since our government is at least ostensibly a government of the people, for the people, and by the people, that the government might take a role in standardizing education in terms of curriculum, teacher standards, and all the rest. We think this would still allow the schools to be run by the people, but without resulting in the anarchy that your plan suggests."

"Yes, I quite understand that position," said Extan. "But we have little trust in systems of government as they presently exist. We think that this would simply enable the system to utilize the schools more effectively in promoting the ends we have already rejected. We realize that the local control we envisage would create additional problems, but we think it would prevent education from being bureaucratized to the extent it is at the present time. We find the amount of control exercized by central powers already intolerable, and we do not think that additional central control will improve the situation."

"I would like to come in at this point since I am also very concerned with who runs the schools," said Pennington. "I agree with the progressivist that the existentialist has not thought out his position on local control fully. To have local control, or control by the people as you put it, would mean that our schools would be run not by professional educators, or even by the intelligent individuals of society, but by people who have little knowledge of education or anything else. I think that your view is very appealing romantically, but it would result in absolute chaos, and those places without chaos would be run on an extremely low level. I personally would favor even more control than the progressivist. I think that we need something very akin to the ministries of education that you find in other countries. The minister of education in France once said that he could look at his watch and tell you what they were doing in every classroom in the country. Although I would favor some amount of flexibility, I think that we should try to set up a school system that is the result of our best thinking in education. You know as well as I do that we have discovered certain things that are important, and certain desirable ways of teaching, but they are not utilized uniformly throughout the country. It is also undesirable in our mobile kind of society for a child to be transferred from one school system to another and find one so incredibly different from the other. I like the idea of a cabinet position for education as the reconstructionist mentioned, and I think that such a person should have great authority to put ideas into motion on a universal scale."

"I am intrigued with this idea of a cabinet position, as well as the centralization you propose, but I wonder," said Extan, "what type of person is going to be in this cabinet position?"

"I would hope," said Pennington, "that he would know something about the history and methods of education, but primarily that he would know a great deal about its philosophy and see that the schools adopt a sensible philosophy of education."

"Then," replied the existentialist, "it is to be something like Plato's philosopher king ruling over the educational enterprise?"

"I don't object to such an analogy," answered Pennington. "What would be wrong with having the best persons in education determine policy instead of what we have at the present time when every parent who reads an article on education considers himself or herself an authority?"

"To begin with," said Extan, "I don't think we know enough about education to say what aims, methods, or philosophy is best, and even if it were best, there is no assurance that it would remain best. I think we would be much better off if we adopted an experimental attitude toward education, as well as life in general."

"I don't object to experimentation," said Pennington, "but I think that when we find some things better than others that we should implement them."

"You are beginning to sound like the progressivist," said Beattie, "in talking about experimentation and implementing things that work better."

"Yes, only our definition of work does not necessarily mean 'what will fit in with contemporary society,' " said Pennington. "We are the tender-minded he talks of who feel that things may work in an aesthetic-philosophical-religious sense as well as in a cold scientific one."

"I object to the phrase 'cold scientific,' " said Price. "Why is science cold? I never thought of it that way myself. Science takes account of emotions and feelings too, and can deal with them much more effectively, I think, than philosophy or religion can. When we talk about the whole child we mean taking these things into account, and we do."

"If I may go on to another point," said Pennington. "We are very much alarmed at the materialism that pervades society and that pervades and is encouraged by education. If you look at your schools, for example, you will see that they not only create people to engineer more materialism, but to buy more products as well. In the elementary grades children are exposed to ads for products in their school newspapers, not to mention the hucksterizing of radio and TV. We would like to see the schools, rather than being perpetrators of this conspiracy, at least serve as a counter force to it, and hopefully to serve in a way that might eventually extinguish it entirely. We would like to think that the minds of young children are being directed somewhere other than toward the mere piling up of possessions which I think do more harm than good. We all know that people these days are rated not in terms of what they are, or in terms of what they know, but in terms of what they have. And the person who has the most material goods or the most money is the best person."

"How do you expect to control this?" asked Reed.

"By the kinds of studies that are taught," replied Pennington. "We think that the humanities by and large put an emphasis on humanity rather than on things or products. Also, we feel that the teacher should have a philosophical-religious orientation toward life, and that this would also serve as a way of orienting people away from the crass commercialism of life."

"I think we all agree that there is too much commercialism," said Extan, "but I am not sure that the way of solving it is to present people with fictionalized ideas of existence which I think most of the classics provide, nor the superstitions of religion. After all, this is reality, like it or not. It doesn't seem to me that presenting ideals is a good way of counteracting it. I think you have to expose what is there for what it is, rather than to try to cover it up with some kind of philosophical varnish."

"I would like to think that people would attack these things," said Pennington, "but I also think you have to present models for people to consider, and I think that the classics provide such models as to what man can and should become."

"That certainly fits in with the idea of utopia," said Reed, "though I would probably be a little less likely than you to say what man or society should become, though I must confess that I do go that far on occasion. If you intend your models as guides to better behavior I would certainly agree with you, though I think models can also be found outside the classics."

"Yes, both of you are other-worldly," said Estabrook, " and therein lies the problem. I personally take a piecemeal approach to the problems of our society in dealing with them one by one within the context in which they exist. I don't think you really get anywhere looking toward the distant future as the reconstructionist does or toward the distant past as the perennialist does. I think you have to face things as they are. I would like to point out that we are not at all satisfied with a lot of things in society, but we don't think you get anywhere by escaping from the problem. Let's be realistic. You must face the way people are and the way the world is, and then go from there. The perennialist talks about bringing the classics into the schools—that we need more in the way of the humanities. But that is exactly what we have had for the bulk of our educational history, and I cannot see where it really has made man more humane or solved the problems he mentioned. In many ways, I think, it blinds people to the problems that exist. We must face the fact that we live in an often hostile world where not everyone is good and beautiful. We essentialists face the fact that things are not perfect in the world, nor do we think they ever will be. We know that laws are not infallible, but we don't feel that people have a right to go around breaking them because they aren't perfect, or because they may be different in the future. We think peace is a good thing, but we would not therefore propose that we do away with all guns and missiles. Man has come a long way, and he has built society slowly. He has made a lot of mistakes, but we think that he has also tried to correct them, and to improve. I think that the humanities served some useful purpose when they gave man a deeper feeling for himself and the universe, but that they are now out of date in terms of more relevant material. I think that the advancement of science served in a large way to diminish this classical influence in education, and I think that by and large the change was beneficial. Science exploded a lot of myths established by classical writers from Aristotle down; not only scientific myths but myths regarding sexuality and society as well. We have progressed by the facts we have painfully and with great difficulty acquired, and we shall painfully progress through the acquiring of new facts. It was Comenius who once proposed that we have a pansophic center where we begin to store all that man has learned. As has already been mentioned, this is now being proposed by Buckminster Fuller who wants to put all of man's knowledge into a giant computer. Just think what advantages this would have. Every individual and every school child could plug into this computer and ask it any fact about the universe and receive an immediate and reliable answer."

"There are only two problems," replied Pennington. "One is that there are a lot of things we believe as theories not facts, and secondly, facts change."

"I realize that," said Estabrook. "But they don't change as much as you imply. Most of the facts we learned in school are still true, despite what the progressivist might say, and there are some that have always been true. We realize that there has to be a margin of error, but the margin gets smaller every day through the more careful verifiability procedures we are developing."

"It has always interested me to observe," said Price, "that although you are interested in preserving what we have, your insistence on facts and on science reminds me very much of the kind of education promoted by the Soviets."

"I am not taken aback by that remark as much as you thought I might be," replied Estabrook. "I think there are similarities in our methods, though not in our aims. It seems important to note too that we do find the same methods useful, and I think this gives additional credence to the idea that we have come to agreement independently about what method is best. We are, of course, somewhat upset that the United States has not seen the use of education as a weapon as the Soviets have. They see very clearly that the future will belong to those who are well trained. I fear that their training, particularly in mathematics and science, is far superior to ours at the present time, and we feel a special need to alert people to the fact that we are in a competitive situation where we cannot afford to fail. We would like to have special schools, for example, where gifted students might pursue subjects far beyond the ordinary curriculum. At the present time we feel that our watered-down curricula, as well as all of these fads and frills that take up necessary school time, are preventing us from developing the full potential that some students have. In our present programs, too, where all students take the same general kind of curriculum, the really good students are held back by the dull and mediocre ones. We would like to see a change in our educational programs so that there is a greater recognition of individual differences, together with the recognition of education as a high priority item in the race between nations."

"I dislike the thought that education is to be used as a weapon when it should be used as an instrument for ending wars and aggression," said Reed.

"I should like to see an end to war also," added Estabrook, "but again, we must be realistic. The United States is engaged in an ideological as well as military race. There are powers whose beliefs we feel are detrimental, and we must face the fact that if we do not marshall our forces in education in ways that deal with such a threat we could be extinguished as a nation. It is not a matter of choice that we should use education for this purpose, it is a matter of necessity."

"This issue of education as a tool in war is not a new one," said Beattie. "When was education not so used? Soldiers have to be trained, the populace must be educated to hate the enemy sufficiently, and then, after the war is over, people must be educated to peace. One might also contend, I think, that education as we know it, also causes wars. We teach people in ways that generate great hostility, and the subjects we teach often extol war and bloodshed. Look at who we label as great men in history. Most of them are generals or military men of some rank. We talk about the American Revolution and the Civil War in the most reminiscent terms, and we award those who kill a lot with medals and other honors. Is it surprising then that men can readily go to war and kill each other when society so honors it? Reward increases the likelihood that the behavior being rewarded will reoccur."

"I should like to say here," said Estabrook, "that the men in these wars you mentioned were fighting for freedom, justice, and democracy, and without their efforts we might not be free today."

"I doubt that very much," replied the behavioral engineer. "We fought against England, and yet England is as free as we are. We had the Civil War, but I rather doubt that it changed things much. Slavery would have disappeared anyway as an inefficient method when machines became so much better. But what I am really attacking here is the heaping of honors upon those who killed or engaged in war. Even if we were to assume that it was a task that needed to be done, which I doubt, why continue to hold it so high; why not consider it an unfortunate necessity and forget it? And yet one can hardly go into any town and not find monuments and other artifacts that remind him of the various wars we have been engaged in. I think that if we want to end war what we have to do is to stop rewarding it, but I see no evidence that we have understood, much less accepted this principle. Actually, the whole process begins in childhood. It is not only our nation that is aggressive, but man in general. Whether man is born aggressive or not I do not care to debate because it does not make any difference. We have a great deal of evidence to show that we can make people aggressive or we can eliminate aggression through the engineering of human behavior. We have experiments, for example, where pigeons are made aggressive by being rewarded for pecking each other. In the same way, if you find a very aggressive individual, you can trace back to the things that made him that way, and I think you will see that it was the rewards and punishments of the system that did it. So with most children. We know that a certain amount of drive is good and we generally reward it. But rewards come from many different places, and although teachers might not reward aggressive behavior, it is generally true that the peer group will, particularly if that peer group feels threatened by the forces it is attacking."

"How, by utilizing rewards, might we then be able to eliminate aggression?" asked Reed.

"When aggressive behavior occurs it should be ignored," stated Beattie. "Unless of course there is some danger involved to those engaged in it. We should also constantly take note of those who do not engage in aggressive behavior, and in particular those who show love and kindness toward others, and reward them. I think, however, that if you look at our society you will see that most people who exhibit love and kindness are punished by being called soft or sissy, or such things as peaceniks and the like. Often, aggressive behavior is rewarded when a child comes home and tells his father that he beat up another child, and the father rewards him by calling him brave or saying that he is standing up for his rights, i.e., is 'a real boy,' and so on. As I was saying before, you can trace people's lives, and I think you will see that those who are aggressive were rewarded for that kind of behavior, and that is why they continue to do it. We are very disturbed by the great use of aversive punishment in society, which we feel leads to further hostility and aggression. Everyday, and in many many ways, we attempt to correct people's behavior by punishing them. And yet we see, over and over again, that it does not work; that the criminal returns to crime, that the punished child continues to repeat what he was punished for, and so on continuously. We see it also in terms of the control of the poor and minority groups where they are punished with the nightstick or with guns, or jail, and again, we see that there is a constant cry for more nightsticks and more guns because it doesn't work. That is one of the most noticeable things in our society, that instead of admitting that aversive punishment does not work, we ask for more of it. TV and the mass media are also greatly to blame in this respect. How does the cowboy obtain justice, or whatever he wants, except through some form of violence? On show after show we see the good guys triumphing not through thinking or love, but through violence. If you imagine the amount of violence on TV, together with the great number of hours that children and adults watch it, is it any wonder that we have the amount of violence in society that we do have?"

"I think that one of the questions in my mind," said Estabrook, "is: Does TV cause the violence, or is it because people want it that it is on TV?"

"I think both," responded Beattie. "I think that children are made hostile by a very repressive home environment, and that TV feeds and caters to the hostile feelings that most people have and therefore aggression continues to feed upon itself. I think, too, that the programs on our TV are getting more violent as time goes on. And yet, I feel that if we were to make changes on TV so that instead of violence we showed people being rewarded for helping each other, we could begin to make significant changes in people's personalities. If we were to follow through with this in the home, the school, and the street, there is no limit to what we could do to bring out loving human beings in less than a generation."

"If everyone were loving and loved his neighbor who would fight our wars?" asked Pennington.

"Yes, you can begin to see the obstacles we should have to face," replied Beattie. "I know that people say that we are not ready for this. I only wish we were. But it does serve to show the hypocrisy in our society when we say we want peace and justice, whereas in reality, directly or indirectly, we promote war and exploitation. I think that one of the things we should try to do is to show that aggression and war, if you examine all the consequences of them, are really unrewarding. We have not yet begun to see this or to teach it to others. But it seems to me that it might be a useful first step in turning people away from the idea of using violence to settle their differences."

"I wonder," said Estabrook, "if we might conclude our discussion by having each one of us comment on the kind of person we would like to see our education system turn out. Also, we might comment on some of the feelings we share with each other in our common concern for education. Why don't we begin again with Pennington?"

"I wish to say," responded Pennington, "that I have greatly enjoyed this opportunity to present my views on education, and I think that I have personally improved my understanding of the other major educational philosophies. I have been made aware, however, that there are serious yet understandable differences that separate us. And while I agree that we should strive to eliminate war, poverty, and injustice, I think there are different ways of going about it. I suppose you might say that we feel that an educated citizenry is the best answer to these solutions; not educated in the sense of being schooled, but educated in the deeper sense of that term, of having one's emotions educated as well as the intellect. We think that many of the problems mentioned here today, such as whether we should or should not condition people against war, are primarily philosophical questions, and I fear that the kind of education we are giving most people is not the kind of education that will enable them to deal with such problems. We are, I think, too concerned with turning out educational technicians who can do a job routinely, yet lack the intellect or the ability to handle problems in any real sense. One of the things that concerns me about progressivism, for example, is not its reliance upon workability, but the question of how we know whether something has really worked or not. We think that in education, as well as in other areas, we are neglecting the fund of wisdom that already exists, and in many ways has already been tested. We are constantly implementing ideas from the past as new things, but because so many people are unfamiliar with the past they are not aware of this fact. To put it plainly, we believe that an educated man should know the past and utilize the past in looking at the present. He would be, in the best sense of the word, philosophical. What I mean by this is not that he would be an ivory-tower philosopher, but that he would look at things synoptically or holistically and try to synthesize their meanings. I think that in the world today, it is not more doers that we need, but more men who understand what they are doing, and this is what we are trying to promote. Now, I'll let the essentialist speak."

"Like the perennialist," said Estabrook, "I am very thankful for the opportunity to present my ideas, and I wish to thank all of you for presenting powerful and cogent arguments for your positions. Let me say that I see some value in all of your views, but my major criticism would be that you do not see reality as it is. Even though the existentialist would maintain that he sees reality more clearly than I do, I think that his view of reality is eclipsed by his great attention on the bad rather than the good side. What we are promoting is an objective look by man at his society and the world. We are a little disturbed because an objective look at mankind leads us to see that nothing that we have, and we have much that is good, will be kept without educational maintenance. We feel that things are not being maintained well at the present, and that we are slipping because our educational system is slipping. To some extent we feel that the fault for this lies upon an erroneous view of what education should be about, and although we might agree with the reconstructionist about the bright future that can be before us, we feel that there will be no future at all if we don't first take care of what we have. We are not defending everything that exists, but we do feel that one shouldn't throw out the good with the bad. We believe that the best change agent is the person who can look objectively at the world and determine the best course of action. I mean by this a person who understands the world, not in any fanciful abstract way, but who understands it concretely. We think that armed with such knowledge a person will become able to deal with reality in ways that provide a sensible and sane direction for society and for mankind. Now, I'll let the progressivist respond."

"Yes, I too have enjoyed our meeting and look forward to other continued debates of this kind," said Price. "I think that they serve a useful purpose not only in allowing others to know what we stand for, but in making us crystallize our own ideas for argument. I wish to say that the kind of person we would like to see the schools turn out would be the kind of person who can face the problems of his life, whether they be emotional, philosophical, social, or educational, and solve them effectively. We feel it is more important to know how to find information than to have it. We also feel that the good problem-solver is better armed for the future than one who may be carrying around outdated philosophies and facts. We have nothing against facts and philosophies per se, but we do feel that the method of gaining knowledge efficiently should be the paramount criterion in evaluating a good educational program. Now, I'll turn you over to the reconstructionist."

"Yes, thank you," replied Reed. "It has been a unique experience for me to be in such brilliant company, and I am very grateful for the opportunity. I think it is quite fitting that I follow the progressivist for certainly we are very close philosophically, and I would certainly promote everything he stands for. Our only contention is that progressivism doesn't go far enough, and we would like to extend these problem-solving operations toward making significant changes in the social structure. To do this we also feel that we need to think more about what kinds of things we want, and then utilize effective methods for bringing these things into being. We are afraid of philosophies like perennialism and essentialism, which we feel harden resistance to change and tend to make men more content with the here and now. We also feel that not to be concerned with the future could be quite deadly, for if we do not frame some adequate direction for dealing with present problems, the problems will soon overwhelm us. We like to think of ourselves as forward-looking agents of change, and we feel that education should be changed in ways that would enable it to turn out more change agents. Now, the behavioral engineer."

"Yes, of course we're concerned with the future too," said Beattie, "as I have stated many times. We would like to see certain hard decisions made as to what needs to be done in our society, and we would like to see the schools implement procedures to bring such things about. We feel that certain philosophical decisions need to be made, but that the process is not one of philosophy but more a technical one. We would like to see man progress toward those values our wisest men have agreed upon, and we would utilize the force of conditioning as a way of bringing this about. We find that your philosophies, as interesting as they are, are really not workable in terms of the major changes that need to be made in man and society. We desire a better future, and we think that problem-solving is simply one facet of education that needs to be further developed and controlled. I should like to say that we are not interested in turning out robots, as some of you have indicated, but we would like to turn out people who are curious, intelligent, have a love of beauty, and if something can be effective enough in doing that, we think of it as an almost ideal educational method. Now, the existentialist."

"I have been listening carefully throughout this debate," said Extan, "and though I have tried to be fair and open-minded, this discussion has made me aware of why a philosophy such as existentialism had to come into being. All of you are concerned with philosophy, facts, problems, the future, conditioning, or what have you, but you seem to be concerned with man very little. We think that man is the one thing you leave out of all your calculations and that this is why we are so badly needed. I am afraid that you treat man as a thing to be manipulated by your methods, and our feeling is that man needs to be freed by you, not imprisoned by stronger bonds than ever before. I get the feeling that if your ideas really become implemented, man will be worse rather than better off. Our approach is not to force man to do any of the things you mentioned, but to make him free so that he may make his own decisions about education and life. We feel that it is important that man be his own master, but we think that most of what passes for education serves to stifle and prevent man from becoming man. If you want to know what we would like to see develop through the process of education, it is individuals, and that is precisely what we are not getting. We are sometimes of the opinion that education does more harm than good, but we have some hope that education is changing in ways that will allow man to express himself more freely, and that such a change will result in happier and more realistically oriented individuals."

Questions for Discussion

1. Are there any examples you can think of to attack or defend Extan's view (p. 83) that intellectuals are no less prone to war, violence, or inhumanity than those who are not?

2. Comment on Price's view that we can measure love or justice in terms of their consequences. (p. 84)

3. Do you agree with Reed (p. 86) that fear of change is a personality problem as much as anything else?

4. Comment on Estabrook's statement (pp. 86–87) that educational texts written fifty years ago are better than their contemporaries.

5. Comment on the list of suggestions made by Reed for improving society. (pp. 92–93)

6. Do you agree with Pennington (pp. 94–95) that "workability" can become as dogmatic a principle as the principles of some religions?

7. Comment on Pennington's concern for the materialism which he feels pervades society and is encouraged by education. (p. 99)

8. Which philosopher's argument did you find to be the strongest? Why?

9. Discuss each of these philosophies in terms of curriculum, ideal teacher, and educational outcome.

Epilogue

After the discussion was concluded all six participants returned to their respective universities. All of them felt wiser for the experience, and there was even a suggestion put forth that such a discussion be held on a yearly basis. Needless to say, such a discussion must be considered in a time context, and future changes in man and society would necessitate a constant reevaluation of all educational philosophies.

EDCO Corporation had its tape, and our philosophers had the experience of real interaction which seldom occurs unless one takes the trouble to set it up. We would like to think that philosophers do this on their own accord, but unfortunately, partisan philosophy exists as much as partisan politics. Hopefully, however, such a debate as this serves to show the value to be gained from putting one's educational philosophy in the arena of discussion, so to speak.

Although many readers may not find any of the six educational philosophies presented here entirely to their liking, there is always the possibility of an eclectic approach whereby one extracts useful parts of each; and some philosophers have referred to themselves as essentialist-pragmatists or progressive-existentialists. Many educationists taking such a view have found important ideas to be considered in each philosophy, and such an eclectic view also serves to diminish dogmatic reliance upon a single educational philosophy for guidance. It is to be hoped that the reader will continue the dialogue in his own mind, and constantly explore new questions and answers.

Educational philosophies differ not only in terms of basic educational beliefs, but also in terms of the kinds of things implied by those beliefs. Not only do varying educational philosophies imply a difference in the kind of curriculum each would promote, but also in terms of such things as seating, exams, architecture, and political posture. The following schematic summary is intended as a way of pointing out such differences.

Educational Philosophy	Root Philosophy	Rationale	Curriculum	Teacher
perennialism	idealism	deals with that which is lasting — stresses intellectual attainment — the search for truth	great books liberal arts	philosophically oriented — knowledgeable about great ideas
essentialism	realism	deals with basic knowledge — facts	3 Rs history science foreign language English	fact oriented — knowledgeable about scientific and technical data
progressivism	pragmatism	search for things that work — experimental — democratic	core flexible revolves around interests and needs student-centered	guide one who can present meaningful problems with skill
reconstructionism	pragmatism	seeks to reconstruct society through education	current events social problems	social activist — utopian oriented
existentialism	existentialism	importance of the individual — "existence precedes essence" — paradox, subjectivity, anxiety	individual preference	committed individual — I-Thou — person who is both teacher and learner — one who provides a free environment
behavioral engineering	behaviorism	controlled behavior through positive and aversive reinforcement	composed of small steps organized systematic data	expert conditioner

Educational Philosophy	Method of Teaching	Exam	Preferred Architecture	Seating	Educational Outcome
perennialism	lecture discussions seminars	essay	classical	students grouped around teacher (philosopher)	philosopher
essentialism	lecture teaching machines	objective	efficient functional	students grouped around teacher (scientist)	technician scientist
progressivism	discussion projects	gauge how well people can problem-solve	flexible natural	group	good problem-solver
reconstructionism	real-life projects action projects	gauge ability as activist	non-school setting "schools without walls"	outside involvement	social activist
existentialism	learner is encouraged to discover the best method for himself	student should learn to examine himself	individual preference	individual preference	inner-directed person "authentic individual" committed involved
behavioral engineering	teaching machines that provide immediate reinforcement	exam that provides immediate reinforcement	conditioned environment	one that provides positive reinforcement	conditioned person

Selected Readings

Perennialism

Adler, Mortimer, and Mayer, Milton. *The Revolution in Education.* Chicago: Univ. of Chicago Press, 1958.

Aquinas, St. Thomas. *The Teacher—The Mind.* Chicago: Henry Regnery Co., 1953.

Butler, J. Donald. *Four Philosophies and Their Practice in Education and Religion,* rev. ed. New York: Harper and Bros., 1957.

Greene, Theodore. *Liberal Education Reconsidered.* Cambridge, Mass.: Harvard University Press, 1953.

Horne, Herman H. *Idealism in Education.* New York: The Macmillan Co., 1910.

Hutchins, Robert M. *Great Books, the Foundations of a Liberal Education.* New York: Simon and Schuster, 1954.

Maritain, Jacques. *Education at the Crossroads.* New Haven, Conn.: Yale University Press, 1943.

Plato. *The Republic.* Oxford, England: The Clarendon Press, 1951.

Essentialism

Bestor, Arthur E. *Educational Wastelands.* Urbana, Ill.: Univ. of Illinois Press, 1953.

Conant, James Bryant. *Education and Liberty.* Cambridge, Mass.: Harvard University Press, 1953.

Koerner, James D. *The Miseducation of American Teachers.* Boston, Mass.: Houghton Mifflin Co., 1963.

Rafferty, Max. *What Are They Doing to Your Children?* New York: The New American Library, 1963.

Rickover, Hyman G. *Education and Freedom.* New York: E. P. Dutton Co., 1959.

Progressivism

Bode, Boyd H. *Progressive Education at the Crossroads.* New York: Newson, 1938.

Childs, John Lawrence. *American Pragmatism and Education.* New York: Holt, Rinehart and Winston, 1956.

116

Dewey, John. *Democracy and Education.* New York: The Macmillan Co., 1916.

———. *Experience and Education.* New York: The Macmillan Co., 1938.

James, William. *Talks to Teachers.* New York: Holt, Rinehart and Winston, 1899.

Kilpatrick, William Heard. *Philosophy of Education.* New York: The Macmillan Co., 1951.

Parker, Francis W. *Talks on Pedagogics.* New York: John Day Co., 1937.

Reconstructionism

Brameld, Theodore. *Education for the Emerging Age.* New York: Harper Bros., 1961.

———. *Toward A Reconstructed Philosophy of Education.* New York: Dryden Press, 1956.

Counts, George S. *Dare the School Build a New Social Order?* New York: The John Day Co., 1932.

Goodman, Paul. *Compulsory Miseducation.* New York: Horizon Press, 1964.

Gutek, Gerald L. *The Educational Theory of George S. Counts.* Columbus, Ohio: Ohio State University Press, 1971.

Mannheim, Karl. *Ideology and Utopia.* New York: Harcourt, Brace, and Co., 1936.

Mumford, Lewis. *The Story of Utopias.* New York: Boni and Liveright, 1924.

Existentialism

Buber, Martin. *I and Thou.* New York: Charles Scribner's Sons, 1958.

Kneller, George F. *Existentialism and Education.* New York: John Wiley, 1958.

Morris, Van Cleve. *Existentialism in Education.* New York: Harper and Row, 1966.

Neill, A. S. *Summerhill.* New York: Hart Publishing Co., 1960.

Sartre, Jean-Paul. *Existentialism and Human Emotions.* New York: Philosophical Library, 1947.

Behavioral Engineering

Bereiter, C., and Engleman, S. *Teaching Disadvantaged Children in the Pre-School.* Englewood Cliffs, N.J.: Prentice-Hall, 1966.

Ferster, C. B. and Skinner, B. F. *Schedules of Reinforcement.* New York: Appleton-Century-Crofts, 1957.

Hilgard, E. R. and Marquis, D. G. *Conditioning and Learning.* New York: Appleton Century Co., 1940.

Pavlov, I. P. *Conditioned Reflexes.* London: Oxford Univ. Press, 1927.

Skinner, B. F. *Cumulative Record.* New York: Appleton-Century-Crofts, 1959.

———. *Walden Two.* New York: The Macmillan Co., 1948.

Biography

Adler, Mortimer (1902–   )
> Collaborated with Robert M. Hutchins in reprinting the Great Books in a complete set and developed the Syntopicon as an index to the ideas of the Great Books. Founder of the Institute for Philosophical Research. *How to Read a Book: The Art of Getting a Liberal Education.*

Andreae, Johann Valentin (1586–1654)
> Born in Germany. A Lutheran pastor who made many significant and educational changes. Very much influenced by the Renaissance and the Protestant Reformation. *Christianopolis.*

Aquinas, Thomas (1225–1274)
> Philosopher of the Middle Ages whose *Summa Theologica* demonstrated the rationality of the universe as a revelation of God.

Aristotle (384–322 B.C.)
> Ancient Greek philosopher who was a Realist. His educational ideas are found mainly in *The Ethics* and *The Politics.*

Augustine, Aurelius Augustinus (353–430)
> Born at Tagaste in Numidia and spent much time in Rome. Became Christian philosopher and saint. *The City of God, Confessions.*

Bacon, Francis (1561–1626)
> Founder of modern inductive logic. *The Advancement of Learning* and *Novum Organum.*

De Beauvoir, Simone (1909–   )
> French existentialist writer and novelist closely associated with Jean-Paul Sartre. *The Mandarins, The Second Sex.*

Bellamy, Edward (1850–1898)
> A journalist who was associated with the *New York Evening Post,* the *Springfield Union,* and the *Berkshire Courier. Looking Backward.*

Bereiter, Carl (1930–   )
> Educator and writer. *Teaching Disadvantaged Children in the Preschool* with Siegfried Engleman.

Berkeley, George (1685–1753)
> An idealist who contended that only spirits and ideas exist. *A Treatise Concerning the Principles of Human Knowledge.*

Bode, Boyd (1873–1953)
Education. *Progressive Education at the Crossroads, How We Learn.*

Bohr, Niels (1885–1962)
Danish physicist. Extended the theory of atomic structure through the quantum theory. *Theory of Spectra and Atomic Constitution. Atomic Theory and Description of Nature.*

Brameld, Theodore (1904–   )
Strong supporter of reconstructionism in education. *Toward a Reconstructed Philosophy of Education, Philosophies of Education in Cultural Perspective.*

Buber, Martin (1878–1965)
Jewish existentialist and theologian. *I and Thou, Between Man and Man.*

Butler, Samuel (1835–1902)
Born in England. A painter and writer who turned for a while to raising sheep in New Zealand. *Erewhon.*

Campanella, Thomas (1568–1639)
A Catholic cleric, charged with attempting to overthrow the Spanish government in Naples and imprisoned for twenty-seven years. *City of the Sun.*

Camus, Albert (1913–1959)
Born in Algeria. French existentialist and writer. *The Stranger, The Myth of Sisyphus, The Plague.*

Childs, John L. (1889–1921)
Supporter of Progressivism in education. *American Pragmatism and Education, Education and Morals.*

Comenius, John Ames (1592–1671)
Czech educational reformer. *The Great Didactic.*

Conant, James Bryant (1893–   )
Has made many suggestions for the renovation of American education, including the "comprehensive high school." *The American High School Today, The Education of American Teachers.*

Counts, George (1889–   )
Author and educator. Presently teaching at Southern Illinois University. *Dare The Schools Build a New Social Order? The Challenge of Soviet Education, Education and Human Freedom in the Age of Technology.*

Cram, Ralph Adams (1863–1942)
An architect who specialized in the construction of ecclesiastical and educational buildings, and was a leading authority on Gothic architecture. *Walled Towns.*

Darwin, Charles (1809–1882)
English discoverer of natural selection. *The Origin of Species by Means of Natural Selection.*

Dewey, John (1859–1952)
Distinguished representative of American pragmatism, particularly as

applied to American education. Books include *Reconstruction in Philosophy, Democracy and Education.*

Engleman, Siegfried (1931–   )
Education specialist. *Teaching Disadvantaged Children in the Preschool* with Carl Bereiter. *Preventing Failure in the Early Grades.*

Faulkner, William (1897–1962)
American author. *The Sound and the Fury, Requiem for a Nun.*

Freud, Sigmund (1856–1939)
Austrian founder of psychoanalysis. *Totem and Taboo, The Future of an Illusion.*

Fuller, Buckminster (1895–   )
Engineer, designer, author, inventor. Discovered energetic-synergetic geometry, geodesic structures, tensegrity structures. *Nine Chains to the Moon, Utopia or Oblivion: The Prospects for Humanity.*

Galilei, Galileo (1564–1642)
Italian astronomer. Proved that falling bodies fall with equal velocity. Confirmed Copernican theory. *Dialogue on the Great World Systems, Two New Sciences.*

Golding, William (1911–   )
English author. *Lord of the Flies, The Inheritors.*

Gott, Samuel (1613–1671)
Born in London. An attorney and writer. Wrote a utopia entitled *Nova Solyma.*

Hegel, Georg Wilhelm (1770–1831)
A philosopher who was an exponent of absolute idealism. *The Phenomenology of Spirit.*

Heidegger, Martin (1889–   )
German existential philosopher. *Existence and Being, What Is Philosophy?*

Hemingway, Ernest (1898–1961)
American author. *A Farewell to Arms, For Whom the Bell Tolls.*

Holt, John (1923–   )
Educator and writer. *How Children Fail, How Children Learn, What Do I Do Monday?*

Hsing-chih, Tao (1891–1946)
Chinese educational reformer. *The Reconstruction of Chinese Education.*

Hume, David (1711–1776)
Scottish philosopher and historian. *Treatise of Human Nature.*

Hutchins, Robert (1899–   )
Former president and chancellor of The University of Chicago. Founder of the Center for the Study of Democratic Institutions. *The Higher Learning in America, Education for Freedom.*

Huxley, Aldous (1884–1963)
> English novelist and essayist. *Chrome Yellow, Brave New World.*

James, William (1842–1910)
> American psychologist and philosopher. Early developer of pragmatism. *The Principles of Psychology, The Will to Believe, The Varieties of Religious Experience.*

Jaspers, Karl (1883–   )
> German existential philosopher. *Reason and Existence, The Future of Mankind, The Way to Wisdom.*

Kant, Immanuel (1724–1804)
> Philosopher who reconstructs thinking by a critical metaphysics. *The Critique of Pure Reason, Critique of Practical Reason.*

Kierkegaard, Søren (1813–1855)
> Danish philosopher and theologian. Promoter of existentialism. *Either /Or, The Concept of Dread.*

Kilpatrick, William Heard (1871–1965)
> Strong supporter of Progressivism and follower of John Dewey. *Philosophy of Education, Education for a Changing Civilization.*

Kneller, George F. (1908–   )
> Educator and author. *Existentialism and Education, Introduction to the Philosophy of Education.*

Koerner, James D. (1923–   )
> Former executive director of the Council for Basic Education. *The Case for Basic Education, The Miseducation of American Teachers.*

Locke, John (1632–1704)
> An empirical dualist in epistemology and metaphysics. Considered the mind at birth to be a blank tablet. *An Essay Concerning Human Understanding, Some Thoughts Concerning Education.*

Machiavelli, Nicolo (1469–1527)
> Italian statesman. *The Prince.*

Marcel, Gabriel (1889–   )
> French philosopher and writer. *To Be and To Have, Philosophical Fragments, The Iconoclast.*

Maritain, Jacques (1882–   )
> French Catholic philosopher and writer. Neo-Thomist. *Education at the Crossroads.*

Marx, Karl (1818–1883)
> German founder of international socialism. *Das Kapital.*

Montessori, Maria (1870–1952)
> Italian doctor and educationist. *The Secret of Childhood, The Absorbent Mind.*

More, Thomas (1478–1535)
> Born in England. Chancellor of the duchy of Lancaster under Henry VIII. Hanged on the scaffold in 1535 for opposing the king's offer to

divorce his wife so that he could marry Ann Boleyn. Canonized as a saint by the Roman Catholic Church in 1935. *Utopia.*

Morris, Van Cleve (1921–   )
Educator and author. Presently Dean, School of Education, University of Illinois at Chicago Circle. *Philosophy and the American School, Existentialism in Education.*

Morris, William (1834–1896)
Born in England. A poet and designer. Strong promoter of socialist ideals and author of *News from Nowhere.*

Neill, A. S. (1883–   )
Headmaster and founder of Summerhill. *Summerhill—A Radical Approach to Childrearing, Freedom—Not License.*

Newton, Isaac (1642–1727)
English scientist and mathematician. Discovered Law of Gravity. *Principia.*

Nietzsche, Friedrich (1844–1900)
German philosopher who believed that the fundamental principle of existence is the will for power. *Thus Spake Zarathustra, Beyond Good and Evil.*

Nobel, Alfred (1833–1896)
Swedish inventor and manufacturer. Invented dynamite.

Orwell, George (1903–1950)
English novelist and essayist. *Nineteen Eighty Four, Animal Farm.*

Owen, Robert (1771–1858)
Born in England. Later became a textile manufacturer in New Lanark, Scotland. Made many significant social and humanistic changes through various labor and social reforms. Later founded an experimental community in Harmony, Indiana. *A New View of Society.*

Pavlov, Ivan (1849–1936)
Russian physiologist. Studied conditioning. *Lectures on Conditional Reflexes, Twenty Years of Objective Study of the Higher Nervous Activity (Behavior) in Animals.*

Peirce, Charles Sanders (1839–1914)
American Philosopher. Pioneer of pragmatism. *Studies in Logic.*

Plato (427–347 B.C.)
Ancient Greek philosopher who believed that the only true reality is in terms of ideas. *The Republic, The Laws.*

Rafferty, Max. (1917–   )
Strong supporter of the essentialist view in education. *Suffer Little Children, What Are They Doing to Your Children?*

Rickover, Hyman G. (1900–   )
Father of the atomic submarine and an outspoken critic of American education. *American Education—A National Failure, Education and Freedom.*

Rogers, Carl. (1902–   )

Roosevelt, Theodore (1858–1919)
Twenty-sixth president of the United States.

Rousseau, Jean Jacques (1712–1778)
French philosopher who promoted a return to nature. *Emile, Social Contract.*

Santayana, George (1863–1952)
Spanish-born American philosopher, poet, and novelist. *The Life of Reason, Scepticism and Animal Faith.*

Sartre, Jean-Paul (1905–   )
French philosopher, dramatist and novelist. Prominent exponent of atheistic existentialism. *Nausea, No Exit, Being and Nothingness.*

Skinner, B. F. (1904–   )
Associated with conditioning and programmed instruction. Considered the father of the teaching machine. *Schedules of Reinforcement, Science and Human Behavior, Walden Two.*

Socrates (469–399 B.C.)
Athenian philosopher. Appears as the major protagonist in Plato's works, notably *The Republic.*

Tillich, Paul (1886–1965)
Former protestant theologian. Lectured at Union Theological Seminary in New York. *The Courage To Be, Systematic Theology.*

Voltaire, Francois Marie Arouet de (1694–1778)
French author. *Candide, Philosophical Dictionary.*

Watson, J. B. (1878–1958)
American psychologist. Leading exponent of behaviorism. *Behavior—An Introduction to Comparative Psychology.*

Wells, H. G. (1866–1946)
An English teacher and journalist. Author of more than one-hundred twenty-six volumes dealing with a variety of subjects. Author of *The Outline of History, A Modern Utopia, Men Like Gods.*